Praise for
Business Skills for Data Scientists

Sound, practical and rich in examples and personal experiences, this book is the advice data and analytics professionals need to close the gap between their technical & business-facing skills. Highly recommended.

Debra Logan, Distinguished Analyst VP, Gartner, Inc

The stereotype of a data scientist is someone who is solely focused on refining algorithms. This excellent book demonstrates that business acumen and change management skills are just as important as modeling expertise. Data-focused practitioners will increase their career success by reading it!

Thomas H. Davenport, Distinguished Professor, Babson College and Visiting Professor, Oxford University. Author of "Competing on Analytics" and "The AI Advantage"

As all seasoned data scientists know, the business-side skills are so commonly a critical missing ingredient—but never before have those skills been spelled out so clearly and thoroughly. This book is a breath of fresh air, one I desperately wish I'd had when I was starting out.

Eric Siegel, Founder of Predictive Analytics World and Author of "Predictive Analytics: The Power to Predict Who Will Click, Buy, Lie, or Die"

This book contains a trove of solid lessons that I wish someone had shared with me early in my career before I had to learn them the hard way. A must-read for those early in their career and a great review for those of us who have been around a while.

Bill Franks, Author, Speaker, and Director, Center for Statistics and Analytical Research, Kennesaw State University

Business Skills for Data Scientists

Practical Guidance in Six Key Topics

David Stephenson, PhD

Business Skills for Data Scientists:
Practical Guidance in Six Key Topics
by David Stephenson, PhD

Published by
David Stephenson, Ph.D.
dstephenson@dsianalytics.com
https://dsianalytics.com

Library of Congress Cataloging in Publication Data
Stephenson, David
Business Skills for Data Scientists: Practical Guidance in Six Key Topics

ISBN: 978-1-7361830-0-7 (softcover)
Library of Congress Control Number: 2021901503

First Edition
Printed in the USA and Europe

Contents

Foreword

John F. Elder IV, PhD

Data science generates phenomenal returns on investment—when it gets all the way to production. In Elder Research's first decade, we took on every problem brought to us, from stock trading and drug discovery to sales forecasting and machine fault diagnosis. The fascinating challenges led to many breakthroughs, exhilarating "Aha!" moments, and happy customers. We met their ambitious goals 90% of the time. But follow-up revealed a disheartening message: a full third of those solutions were never implemented, despite the huge ROI they would have provided. Some mysterious "soft" factor was causing rejection, and it was three times riskier than technical failure (30% versus 10%). What was going wrong, and what could be done?

If only we'd had David Stephenson's book then! It is a succinct collection of the lessons I wish our team had known earlier. David here reveals to data scientists how to orient themselves in a business environment, how to thrive in the nontechnical aspects of their careers, and especially how to communicate well with others. Topics are ordered in chapters as you're likely to need them. David describes the types of people, business roles, cultures, goals, and expectations that you'll need to be aware of to navigate office politics and achieve project success—in ways that will resonate with those who analyze distributions of data points in high-dimensional spaces. He provides great tips for successful storytelling using presentations and graphs, and for getting the message right by knowing your audience, your goals, and the hierarchy of your findings. Always, the emphasis is on finding the truth in the data, communicating it clearly, earning trust, and adding value to everyone around you. This is extremely career enhancing, to say the least, and I repeatedly agreed with his many practical suggestions. I found most interesting all the brief stories David shared from his own career to illuminate a point on almost every page.

I think of a data point as being a story in numerical form. A model combines and smooths many points into one "super story." Models are more powerful by far than single stories, but they don't resonate as well. We humans seem to be tuned for stories. We yearn to make sense of the world and naturally store and transmit wisdom as legends and proverbs. Worthy teaching uses both levels, and *Business Skills for Data Scientist*s does a great job of balancing the big picture (model) with memorable specifics.

Back to my own story … To improve our acceptance rate, we studied our own past success and failure cases (i.e., we used data science on ourselves). We learned that what was obvious to us (use our model!) represented a big, scary change to the client, so we had to learn how to help others manage change positively. (We picked up the hard way what wise readers should gather the easy way through this book.) Our efforts worked: in our second decade, project acceptance soared from 60% to 90%. We still have a lot to learn, and this book will help—especially in efficiently propagating the lessons. David has artfully distilled a great deal of practical wisdom tailor-made to address potential blind spots for very bright analysts. I'm eager to use *Business Skills for Data Scientists* as the text for a "Consulting 101" module for my younger colleagues, to help them fully thrive in this fantastic field of data science.

— John Elder IV founded Elder Research, a data science and machine learning consulting firm, in 1995. He is a frequent keynote speaker, inventor of several breakthrough techniques, and coauthor of books on data mining, ensembles, and text mining—two of which received book-of-the-year awards. Dr. Elder served for five years on a panel appointed by President Bush to guide technology for national security.

Preface

Several years ago, a contact who was leading a data science consultancy reached out to me for help developing a training program for high-potential data scientists. Although he could easily cover the technical topics, he needed someone with the right experience to teach the business skills these data scientists would need—soft skills such as communication, collaboration and expectations management.

This was the beginning of an extended collaboration, first with his company, then with additional organizations, and eventually with a leading European business school. Together, we developed and refined the topics and content to train for the business skills we felt were most critical for practicing data scientists.

There's a saying, "In the land of the blind, the one-eyed man is king." In giving those first trainings years ago, I was that one-eyed man. Although I graduated from Cornell with advanced degrees in probability theory, operations research and computer science, what has had the greatest impact on my work in the twenty years I've been working have been the lessons my projects have taught me in the areas of communication, empathy, project management, and building trust. Not only are such business skills required to thrive and produce value outside academia, they're also critical for enabling data scientists to earn more responsibility and eventual promotion.

Over the years, I've continued to develop and refine this business skills curriculum as I've trained hundreds of data scientists within dozens of organizations. I've incorporated additional sources and content, taking into account suggestions and feedback from students and peers.

A number of analytics leaders have told me that the data science industry needs a book on this topic. Business skills are equally as important as, or arguably even more than, advanced technical skills to the success of a data scientist's career. Although myriad books have been written covering various machine learning techniques and programming languages, there is very little material about the business skills necessary for the unique situation in which data scientists find themselves. They need to bridge the gap between cutting-edge technology and practical business needs while navigating a gray area between hype and reality, and work with colleagues who only vaguely understand what data science could or should deliver.

Despite the need, I put off writing such a book for some time. Remembering the amount of time it took me to complete my previous book,[1] I was hesitant to embark on the next "journey of a thousand miles." On March 12, 2020, however, the Netherlands declared its COVID-19 lockdown, and life shifted to a lower gear. This seemed to be the time to finally put a portion of the trainings I'd been developing into book form, the result of which is the book you are holding.

This is also something of a personal memoir. Nearly every topic in this book introduces an area in which I've learned lessons the hard way. I share some of those personal stories in the text (with names and details altered for confidentiality).

---

[1] Stephenson, D. (2018). *Big data demystified: How to use big data, data science and AI to make better business decisions and gain competitive advantage.* Financial Times Press.

Introduction

Being a data scientist,[2] as it turns out, is a lot more complicated than you and I had realized when we were taking courses in machine learning (ML) and programming. Once we started working, we found it was not actually the algorithms or the coding that was so complicated.

Instead, it was the business aspects of our jobs—the nontechnical competencies and organizational savvy that we didn't cover in our coursework—that turned out to be difficult for us. And for data scientists, business skills are the most critical to success in non-academic settings.

In my own career, as I have managed, trained and worked alongside hundreds of data scientists over the past two decades, I don't remember ever hearing a complaint that the algorithms were too difficult. However, I've often listened as data scientists described struggles within the workplace—getting burned by office politics, being assigned mind-numbingly boring tasks, aiming at moving targets, or working with unclear expectations from leadership.

On the flip side, I've also listened to business executives and senior managers moan, in private, about how their data scientists are not effectively communicating, managing projects, relating to stake-holders, or building trust. They've lamented the difficulty of hiring data scientists who are able to produce business value and work well with colleagues.

---

[2] I use the term *data scientist* as an umbrella term for statistics, operations research, business analytics, machine learning, etc. The term *scientist* nicely communicates the degree of innovation and uncertainty surrounding our work.

Business skills can make or break your career. In this book, I cover the skills that I've seen to be most critical for data scientists. This book is based partly on my own experience as a data scientist working across a wide range of countries and industries, partly on principles from professional publications, and partly on input I've received from the hundreds of data scientists who have attended my business skills training sessions in recent years.

The topics I cover in the following twelve chapters will have a significant impact on the success of your career. Each chapter introduces basic principles in one key area, but be aware that entire books have been written on the subjects of some of these individual chapters. I'll generally recommend additional references as appropriate. Think of this book, then, as an overview of key topics and a point of entry for further learning where you need it.

The six topics in this book—company, colleagues, communication (storytelling), expectations, results and careers—are covered in six sections. They are presented roughly in the order you'll need them during your career, with project leadership skills coming later in the book. The final topic, careers, will be relevant at all stages of your career, even as you pursue your first job as a data scientist.

The first section, **company**, will help you work within a larger organization. Chapter one discusses how organizations generally view data scientists, why they hire them and what they expect from them. This chapter begins to explain how you as a data scientist can produce business value, a topic that is more fully developed in chapter ten. Chapter two describes how to relate to the diverse range of individuals within your organization. By understanding how various roles and functions differ in their goals and values, you will be better prepared to deliver valuable results to them.

The second section, **colleagues**, covers interpersonal challenges that often present significant problems for data scientists—cultural misunderstandings, negotiating through disagreements, and office politics. Younger data scientists generally perceive these topics as less important, until the day when they suddenly find them extremely important.

The third section, **storytelling**, covers principles and methods key to oral and visual presentations. This section describes how to clarify your message, which is easy in principle but difficult in practice, and how to produce clear slides, graphs and tables. It goes into detail on techniques for decluttering and drawing focus, leveraging principles such as Gestalt and preattentive processing. The two chapters in this section are perhaps the most immediately relevant for many data scientists and will provide you with some very quick wins, as I've seen from the responses of my training participants.

The fourth section, **expectations**, covers techniques for setting expectations, kicking off a project, and maintaining the trust of your stakeholders. In particular, I cover ways to build consensus at the start of a project and ways to avoid the common mistake of working hard to build a solution that no one wants to use.

The fifth section, **results**, presents principles, techniques, and case studies related to selecting the most beneficial data science projects. It then describes concepts and frameworks that will help you run those projects to successful completion, despite the shifting expectations and lack of clarity so prevalent in data science projects.

The sixth and final section, **careers**, addresses questions I'm often asked by data scientists, such as how to choose between job opportunities, how to strengthen your CV, and even whether to start working independently as a freelance data scientist.

I've resisted the urge to include definitions for terms such as *MVP, KPI, stakeholder,* etc., within the text, but such terms (indicated in bold at their first occurrence) are defined in a glossary at the end.

Despite the wide range of topics covered in this book, there is one central theme. The foundation for all skills I will discuss is **the skill of understanding the perspectives of people around you**, especially the people with whom you, as a data scientist, have the least in common. This foundational skill is often called *empathy*. Understanding the perspectives of the diverse range of colleagues you work with will help you relate more effectively in a business setting, ultimately enabling you to deliver successful data science projects with real business impact.

Company

CHAPTER ONE

Finding Your Place in the Company

I can recall my earlier experiences and moments of frustration.
My colleagues and I kept asking ourselves questions like
'Why did they hire us?' and 'Why is this happening?'
– Andrey S. (data scientist since 2014)

Perhaps you're currently in a role where it's clear to you why you were hired and what your organization expects from you. But many data scientists aren't so lucky. I've spoken with quite a number of data scientists who struggle to find their purpose in the organization or to identify areas where they can add value.

Why do data scientists often end up in roles with no clear direction?

Companies sometimes hire data scientists and invest in expensive technologies because they see others around them doing the same, and so they may start hiring with no clear vision in mind. This lack of vision impacts junior data scientists the hardest, as they haven't yet developed the experience necessary to form their own business goals or define their own place within the organization.

This chapter explains how data scientists generally fit within organizations and how you as a data scientist can best start producing value, even if the people around you aren't sure what to expect from you.

First, let's look at what may have motivated your company to create the role for which you were hired, including what they expected from the role and how they justified the expense. Understanding the perspectives of the decision makers and the factors affecting their decision to bring a data scientist on board will help you interpret the context you find yourself in when you show up for work at a new job.

Why You Were Hired

Companies hire data scientists for three primary reasons:

1. **To complete tasks required by laws and regulations**
   For example, banks and insurance companies are typically required to provide certain solvency calculations.

2. **To continue projects with proven worth**
   Certain industries have long relied on specific analytic methods with proven business value. Examples include fraud detection and credit scoring for banks and crew scheduling for airlines.

3. **To explore new areas of value**
   Here is where we've seen explosive growth over the past decade. Companies such as Google and Amazon have convinced the business community that data science is valuable, and perhaps indispensable, for a business to stay competitive. Many executives believe there's value in data science but don't clearly understand why or how.

What I've observed in the past few years is that most freshly minted data scientists end up being hired for this third reason. This puts them in a precarious position, as they are often unsure what they should work on (as are the people who hired them). Job postings list skills that are ultimately not used, and the new hires themselves quickly grow disillusioned.

If you're fortunate enough to have been hired into a team with an experienced manager and a clear focus on how to achieve business value, you have a great chance of thriving in your role. But even if you aren't so fortunate, and even if you need to set your own focus and prove your value to the people around you in new and unexpected ways, don't worry. One of the primary goals of this book is to show you how to do this.

How You're Being Funded

You'll find perhaps the strongest clue as to why you were hired if you happen to know who in your organization allocated funding for your salary. I talked about the purpose for which you may have been hired. Now let's take a moment to consider how funding works.

Although you may not know for certain what has motivated the organization to set aside funds to hire you and your fellow data scientists, it's likely to be one of several common reasons:

1. **A top-down directive to build data science capabilities**
   It's quite possible the supervisory board "recommended" that the CEO start a data science program. In that case, you're being funded as a strategic initiative, and your real job is to make your leaders look like they're doing their job in "using data science."

2. **Room for innovation in someone's budget**
   Corporate budgets are often "use it or lose it," and managers who don't use up their allocated budget in the current year risk receiving a lower budget the following year. It works similarly for managers with open roles in their team. The

manager may rush to fill the role before it's taken away. Sadly, your funding may be a way to burn up someone's budget in a glorious blaze of hopeful innovation, with your primary deliverable being reports and/or **proofs of concept (POCs)**. This is especially relevant for data science consultants, who can be brought in for just a few months.

3. **A concrete business opportunity**

   In the best scenario, a company brings in data scientists to address clear business applications that have already been identified. In many of the projects I've worked on, we first identified machine learning challenges for which we didn't yet have sufficient staffing. We then hired data scientists with the expectation that they would work on specific projects we anticipated would directly increase revenue or decrease costs. I'll talk more about the methodology for this in chapter nine.

   This third situation is ideal, as your goals, **KPIs** and business value are clear to all, and your work is most likely to survive future budget discussions.

Be aware also that many companies are happier to pay external consultants than they are to hire full-time employees, despite the extra cost. This is particularly the case in Europe, where strict employment laws make laying off employees very difficult. It's also the case for publicly listed companies, where the number of permanent employees reflects negatively on financial statements. Companies also like to hire consultants for projects in which they can be designated as a **capital expense** rather than an **operational expense**.

All this is to say that it's easy for data scientists to stress themselves out wondering why certain budgeting decisions are made or why they were hired but aren't being fully utilized. Sometimes you just need to recognize that the company's budgeting decisions related to data science will be shrouded in mystery. Unless you have insider knowledge—which you typically won't—you'll just need to do your best work and focus on adding value wherever you can, even if it's never clear to you why you were hired.

Of course, most data scientists who find themselves in a position with no clear goals will soon look for a new job. I'll come back to this in chapter twelve.

What to Do If You're Not Given Clear Goals

As you can see, it's quite likely you'll find yourself in an ambiguous role at some point, especially early in your career. If you do find yourself without knowledgeable leadership and with no clear mandate, my advice is this:

1. **Identify what's currently important to your organization.** At a high level, the four areas of application you might see are **cost reduction, revenue increase, market share** and **risk reduction**. Make sure you focus on the one or two that are highest priority, or your projects will not go far. For example, if your organization has just received series C funding (investment for rapid expansion), you'll want to focus on growth metrics, not cutting costs.

   Once you've identified a specific focus area, research how data scientists in other organizations are addressing similar challenges. I'll talk more in chapter ten about identifying valuable data science projects that are aligned with the goals and strategy of your organization.

2. **Actively grow your external network.** Find data scientists working in similar industries and learn how they've been able to deliver business value. Social media is a good way to make

new connections, but in-person events are best for detailed discussions, as people will share more freely in person. Get involved with local data science meetups and see if your company supports attendance at international conferences.

3. **Actively grow your internal network and identify the colleagues most open to working with you.** It's more important that you find the right business partners than that you find the right project, as your business partners will more significantly determine your likelihood of success. In your first days and weeks with the organization, you'll typically be introduced to a broad spectrum of colleagues. Try to get introduced to even more. When your manager mentions someone in a role that you think could be interesting, ask for an introduction: a meeting, an email, or even a simple point across the room.

   As you speak with each person, ask about their work and current projects. Think how they might benefit from your skills, but don't speak up too quickly. Introduce yourself briefly, focusing on the parts of your background that seem most relevant to them in their current situation. If you sense enough interest, ask if they'd like to sit together later to discuss it further. When you have more time with them, focus on understanding their needs and pain points. What do they value and what's making their lives difficult? Take notes, but don't make promises yet.

4. **Work to produce value quickly.** One of the best ways to do this is by focusing first on descriptive and diagnostic analytics, the first two stages of the Gartner Analytics Model described below. Your data skills enable you to link and explore data in ways that most of your colleagues can't or don't—illuminating

new insights that can be extremely useful for your company. I've witnessed the CEO of a midsized company get so excited by a simple chart produced by a new data scientist that he hung that chart on the cafeteria door for everyone to see.

As you start to become familiar with your company's data, look for business insights within that data and dig for answers when the data raises a question that could be interesting from a business perspective. For example, by linking sales and customer data, you might identify a certain customer segment with an unusually high churn rate. Or you might notice an unusual peak in activity and be motivated to dig deeper to understand the cause.

I've mentioned that the first two stages of the Gartner Analytics Model are especially helpful in producing quick wins. Now I'll present all four stages and illustrate them within a multistaged example.

The Gartner Analytics Ascendancy Model

When talking about where data scientists bring value, I find it helpful to refer to the Gartner Analytics Ascendancy Model,[3] which groups analytic projects into four categories:

1. Descriptive—What happened?
2. Diagnostic—Why did it happen?
3. Predictive—What will happen?
4. Prescriptive—How can we make it happen?

I've discussed this model in my previous book,[4] so I won't go into detail here—except to say that the first two categories, descriptive and

---

[3] Hostmann, B. (2012, March 27). *Best practices in analytics: Integrating analytical capabilities and process flows*. Gartner.

[4] Stephenson. *Big data demystified*.

diagnostic, focus on collecting and manipulating data, whereas the last two, predictive and prescriptive, are where the more advanced machine learning methods come into play.

Whereas data scientists generally want to dive straight into the more advanced stages—using machine learning methods—the foundations of data science are laid in the descriptive and diagnostic stages. In fact, a great deal of the real business value come from these two stages.

In my trainings, I often describe how these four stages played out in one of my past consulting projects:

Stage 1: My client observed that they were not meeting forecasted sales figures. This was descriptive analytics: simply collecting the data required to make an observation.

Stage 2: We collected and joined various data sources, created charts and pivot tables, ran analysis, and concluded that the revenue shortfall was caused by insufficient supply of a key product. This was diagnostic analytics.

Stage 3: Once we had identified the reason for the budget shortfall, we set about predicting when we might again see demand outstrip supply for this or other products. This was predictive analytics, an area that often requires more advanced machine learning techniques.

Stage 4: Once we were able to forecast periods and items where demand might exceed supply, we were able to consider how to optimize our pricing strategy to maximize revenue during those periods. This was prescriptive analytics.

Most of the "glory" of data science focuses on the techniques employed in predictive and prescriptive analytics. But not only are these last two stages more difficult, they also bring a much higher risk of failure. In addition, it is often impossible to skip directly to these stages without working through the first two.

My suggestion to young data scientists is to focus on the descriptive and diagnostic analytics, at least initially. Even though the techniques are basic, you'll be amazed at how much enthusiasm the results will generate. Providing basic business insights using descriptive and diagnostic analytics will almost certainly win you substantial credibility within the business. Starting out by trying to implement advanced ML methods, on the other hand, will very likely earn you little thanks and ultimately end in failure.

First build the foundation, understand the data, earn credibility. Then move on to the cool stuff.

What Determines If a Model Is "Good"?

When we do get to the "cooler" tasks of predictive and prescriptive analytics—the machine learning models—we still need to think carefully about how to produce models that our organizations are "happy" with. Although we data scientists may focus on improving technical ML metrics such as **precision** and **accuracy**, our non-technical colleagues will evaluate our models in other ways. Before you embark on building your first model, be aware of nontechnical model attributes that your colleagues value and often require in machine learning models. Let's start by looking at what you're likely to see in a nontechnical model checklist.

Model Checklists

As organizations mature in their adoption of machine learning, they increasingly require ML applications to meet certain usability requirements, regardless of how well the models perform technically.

In particular, organizations are increasing their use of machine learning models within critical business functions. They're also using greater amounts of personal data—data that is, in turn, becoming more heavily protected by regional and national laws. And some machine learning applications have a far-reaching impact on large populations.

It's no surprise, then, that we're seeing a greater mandate within organizations for monitoring the practical, ethical and legal aspects of machine learning models.

In a survey of over 11,000 data experts, conducted in June, 2018,[5] O'Reilly media asked participants which business-focused model features were a part of their model-building checklist. Here are the top responses:

Feature	Percentage
Explainability and Transparency	65%
Compliance	48%
User Control Over Data and Models	45%
Privacy	43%
Fairness and Bias	40%

Figure 1. Most often cited business-focused features on model checklists

Notice the heavy emphasis on explainability and transparency, features that are important not only for earning end-user trust but also for compliance with Europe's **GDPR** (e.g., in models for insurance premiums or credit scores). We also see an emphasis on producing fair and unbiased models, with the percentage rising to 54% for respondents at advanced stages of ML adoption.

Such model features may not be top of mind for you as a data scientist, but they will be for some of your most important **stakeholders**. If you don't understand and incorporate your company's requirements with respect to such features, your model simply won't be accepted.

---

[5] Source: Lorica, B., & Nathan, P. (2018). *The state of machine learning adoption in the enterprise.* O'Reilly Media.

Evaluating Success

Beyond basic model features, such as the ones listed above, data scientists think about what constitutes a "successfully fit model" differently from how others might think of it. Within our data science teams, we'll talk about how our models perform in terms of **MSE, MAPE, recall, F1 score,** etc., but these terms will generally mean nothing to our nontechnical colleagues. Our colleagues will care about optimizing business metrics—revenue, cost, churn rate, and return on investment—and about any potential negative effect from the models, such as existence of model bias against subpopulations, impact of misclassification (e.g., **type 1 or 2 error**), or business risk in the case of unexpected model failure.

Data scientists are increasingly stepping in line with their colleagues as they measure the success of their models in terms of business goals. In the 2018 O'Reilly survey referenced above, participants were also asked which metrics their organizations were using to evaluate project success. As illustrated below, business metrics were by far the most prevalent.

Figure 2. Metrics most commonly used to evaluate project success

It's interesting to note that over half of respondents did not respond that they were using ML metrics. Although business and ML metrics often move in the same direction, if you wish your work to be understood and appreciated, it's important to prioritize and communicate in terms of the business metrics.

The more quickly you can develop an understanding of your business environment and your company's key business metrics, the faster you'll be able to start delivering value. And aligning your efforts and communication with the way your colleagues think and speak about data will save you time and wasted effort (more on this in future chapters). It may even save your career from foundering when you encounter barriers or bottlenecks in promoting your data science applications—and you will. Unfortunately, such obstacles are common and affect the success of our profession as a whole. Being aware of them can help you to understand the context you're working within so you can act quickly to overcome them.

Obstacles in Delivering Value with Data Science

Despite our enthusiasm to develop and deploy data science techniques, the reality is that our work often encounters one or more obstacles, some of which prove fatal. Although many of these are technical, many—perhaps most—result from a failure to successfully navigate our business environment. The next figure shows a ranking of the most commonly reported "bottlenecks to AI adoption," as reported in a 2019 O'Reilly survey of 1,300 analytics professionals.[6]

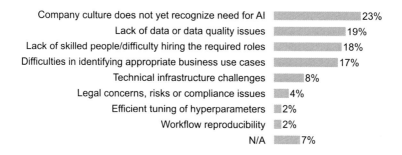

Figure 3. Main bottlenecks to AI adoption

---

[6] Source: Lorica, B., & Nathan, P. (2019). *AI adoption in the enterprise: How companies are planning and prioritizing AI projects in practice.* O'Reilly.

You'll see that three of the top four bottlenecks are related to business skills: convincing our colleagues ("company culture …"), hiring staff, and identifying **use cases**.

The O'Reilly paper also shows that, as companies mature in their use of AI, the first and third of these bottlenecks decrease in prominence, with data issues moving to the lead. However, even in these more mature companies, the task of identifying appropriate business cases remains one of the biggest obstacles. I'll talk about addressing this challenge in chapter ten. For now, let's look at the number one bottleneck listed in Figure 3, which translates to persuading colleagues that they need what you can offer. In particular, let's talk about how to create something that your colleagues will want to use.

Ten Guidelines for Producing Value with Data Science

Because so many people don't recognize the value that data science can bring, you'll need to find straightforward ways to convince your colleagues that your work is both relevant and valuable. Here is a list of factors to consider when striving to accomplish this:

1. **Start by winning trust.**

   As you begin an assignment with new colleagues, don't assume they will trust that you can deliver value. Instead, consciously work to convince them that they can trust both your business understanding and the quality of your work.

   Your first goal should be to listen and learn. Your colleagues should see your desire to understand their work—including their ambitions and pain points—and to learn about the subject matter at hand. Ask insightful questions that demonstrate your understanding and interest.

   Double- and triple-check your work before presenting it, especially at the beginning. Try to deliver first results quickly, whether it be initial analysis of a subset of data or perhaps a proof of concept for a model. Aim to have something to show within two to three weeks, at most. Doing so will allow you to demonstrate your skills sooner rather than later.

2. **Focus on the needs of the moment.**
   There are a lot of good ideas and exciting data science projects you may choose to work on, but watch for what's important in the larger organization at the moment, and pick a project that fits. This will increase your odds of getting support from both management and other departments. And make sure your initiative is aligned with corporate strategy. If the company focus is on growth and expansion, you probably should focus on ways to help marketing and sales rather than on techniques for cost-reduction.

3. **Choose the right format for your deliverable.**
   Know your end user or stakeholder. As a data scientist, what you consider your ideal deliverable is probably a Python notebook, or possibly code deployed as a **web service**. Your end user may instead be expecting a simple Excel tool that they can run on their PC, or a dashboard in their **business intelligence (BI)** interface. Your IT department may be expecting Java code rather than Python. Your primary stakeholder may be expecting a PowerPoint presentation summarizing your results. (I'll come back to this point in chapter eight.)

4. **Meet required standards.**
   If you're producing code meant to be run in a production environment, it will need to meet agreed technical standards. If you're working with customer data, you'll often need to get

signoff from your privacy officer. If you're preparing data for finance, you'll need to meet their standards for accuracy, consistency and timeliness. It's critical to understand and meet the various requirements of your stakeholders. I'll elaborate on this in chapter two.

5. **Match the current appetite for risk, uncertainty and change.** As a data scientist, you will want to move fast (and possibly even break things). But many of your stakeholders will want to have a solid overview of where you're going and what the risks are. If they feel uncomfortable with the level of uncertainty you're introducing, they may try to put the brakes on your project. I'll come back to this point when I talk about uncertainty avoidance in chapter three.

6. **Match the political environment.** Be sensitive to recent communications from leadership, to the current atmosphere within your organization, and to events that may impact individuals with whom you work. For example, if layoffs have been announced within a department, those colleagues may be less receptive to an unproven data science initiative. Or it may be that you were chosen to lead an initiative that your colleague had wanted to lead, in which case you'll probably have difficulty getting support from that colleague. I'll expand on this in chapter five.

7. **Find gatekeepers who are likely to champion your project.** Your choice of projects depends as much on the availability of internal champions as it does on actual project potential. I'll talk more about this in later chapters.

8. **Make yourself a thought partner rather than a data monkey.**

   Don't fall into the trap of simply accepting small projects to collect data or perform basic analysis, only to deliver results and be given yet another small project. Instead, look to understand the question behind the question. Ask something like, "What's the bigger question you're hoping to answer with this data you've asked me for?" Talk this through with the stakeholder before starting your work.

9. **Prepare opinions and suggestions to deliver along with your analysis.**

   You'll need to determine if and when it's appropriate to share your thoughts, but you should be ready with this input. The process of forming your own opinion will also inspire you to collect additional, unsolicited data and conduct analysis that you anticipate will be helpful. Your stakeholder will generally value your initiative.

10. **Always do a "smell test."**

    Step back and ask yourself if the numbers make sense intuitively. It's easy to leave out a decimal place and suddenly have a number that should be in the thousands become several million. This is one of the fastest ways to lose credibility.

As I mentioned, I'll elaborate on certain elements of the above list throughout this book, while adding more detailed guidance in areas that aren't quite as simple to summarize in single paragraphs.

In Conclusion

Although we data scientists have the potential to provide tremendous value to the companies for which we work, we often struggle to recognize how. Often, we aren't even certain why an organization brought us onboard. There are several levels at which we can provide valuable analysis and a choice of goals we can work toward, so we need to carefully consider both what will bring the most business value and what is most promising from a technical perspective. To have our work accepted, we'll also need to attend both to nontechnical model checklists and to additional expectations of diverse stakeholders.

In this chapter, I've discussed some of these challenges and provided advice for navigating the most common roadblocks facing us when we set out to deploy our expertise in a business environment.

In the next chapter, I'll explain how to better understand various roles and responsibilities within your organization, and how this understanding can greatly increase the value you bring as a data scientist.

CHAPTER TWO

Understanding Your Company

When you join a company as a new hire, the first thing you'll need to grasp is what your role is—why you were hired. The second is the context in which you'll be working—how to relate to other departments and to higher levels of management. Because data science is a relatively new field, still working to demonstrate its value in different areas, you'll need to meet your colleagues where they are, rather than expecting them to understand your ways of working. This requires you to build a solid understanding of your company—how your various colleagues work and what is important to them.

The challenge here is that your colleagues can be very diverse. What may be important to one type of colleague is often completely different from what is important to one in a different role or position.

This is why I stress to data scientists the importance of continually striving to understand the people around them, especially those with whom they have the least in common. Without this mindset, a data scientist will not succeed in delivering business value, regardless of technical skill. This chapter will give you a foundational understanding of key roles and positions typically seen within companies, along with advice regarding how you as a data scientist can best relate to them. I'll generalize a bit in this chapter, so it will be up to you to observe how your company operates and what's important to your own colleagues.

When you leave academia, not only will your own goals and pace of work need to change, but so will the cadence and style of your internal communications with colleagues. The first part of this chapter will introduce you to the basic level of understanding you'll need if you're going to adapt. In particular, I'll broadly describe three areas in which our nontechnical colleagues differ from data scientists—their definitions of success, their values, and their working environments—and how you should adjust your ways of working accordingly.

In the second part of the chapter, I'll take a step back and look at the organization as a whole—how it's structured, the hierarchies and where you as a data scientist may fit in.

Variety of Colleagues

Definitions of Success (Goals)

Let's first take a moment for introspection. Ask yourself, "As a data scientist, what is my definition of success?"

Or think of it this way: Imagine it's Friday evening, and you're telling your friends what a great week you just had at work. What would your week have looked like if you were saying this?

As a data scientist, I'd probably say that a good week was when I was able to deploy a new algorithm, or try a new Python package, or when I finally understood some technique I'd been hearing about. My definition of success would be related to pushing boundaries, creating something new—something that almost certainly wasn't perfect, but was, in some sense, groundbreaking.

We understand our own perspective. We've dedicated months, probably years, to building our technical skills, and our definition of success involves using those skills. But to our colleagues, success probably means something completely different.

The reality is that your non–data-science colleagues may not have even heard of deep learning. They're not interested in hearing why Julia is such a better programming language. Even your manager may be perfectly happy with linear regression as a solution.

Now change the question. Imagine your non–data-science colleagues are also sitting with their friends on that Friday evening, talking about their great weeks. What would have made their weeks "successful"?

Start with your colleague in the finance department. At the end of every quarter, their team works weekends to prepare quarterly earnings reports. Success for them means that every report and data field is available on time and that every number adds up exactly to what it should, to the decimal. If there is a small inconsistency in the database, that could translate to another night working until 2:00 a.m. To that colleague, 99% accurate means 100% wrong.

And how about the system administrator down the hall who's responsible for network security? What did their "successful week" look like? Ultimately, it was a week when nothing went wrong. No risks were taken. Permissions were only granted when they fit the regulations and guidelines. Oh, and the data scientist who requested root access or special access rights? They successfully stopped that renegade.

But what about your colleagues in marketing? They're given massive amounts of money to spend on advertising. (Some companies have annual marketing budgets in the billions of dollars.) And yet marketing effectiveness is notoriously difficult to measure, so "success" for them is simply knowing the impact of their marketing efforts. If we as data scientists can give any additional insights or recommendations into optimizing marketing spend—even a rough estimate—they'll be thrilled.

These are just a few illustrations of how your colleagues have different definitions of success. Many of these examples will seem unnatural to you but will seem obvious to your colleagues in their roles.

Values

Just as we have different measures of success, we also place value on different capabilities and ways of working.

Now ask yourself, "What's the sign of a second-rate data scientist?"

Or think of it this way: Imagine a new colleague joins your team, and something about their skills or way of working is not what you think it should be. What might make you feel this way?

As a data scientist, you probably respect colleagues who are proficient with certain machine learning libraries, or who write efficient code, or who can quickly tell what model would be most appropriate for an application. You might quickly lose respect for a colleague who asked a technical question you thought was obvious, or who took too long to do a basic analytic task.

Your colleagues also value skills and ways of working, but what they value may differ significantly. In fact, what they value may be so different as to seem completely unreasonable to you.

Some won't respect you if you don't communicate in a way they feel is professional. Some will expect well-polished presentations, utilizing corporate fonts and color schemes. Some will expect conversations to be friendly and social, and others will want open dialogue with no punches pulled. Some will value precision, and some will value creativity.

What your colleagues value varies more than you might expect, and these perspectives are often deeply ingrained, making them even more powerful and difficult to put aside. This fact makes it all the more important to recognize the core values that direct the goals and opinions of your colleagues.

Working Environment

Even the way we process our workload and prioritize our time differs with our function and with our seniority level.

Ask yourself, "How many things do I need to worry about at work this week?"

At the start of my career, I'd sometimes focus on one model for weeks or months on end. If someone sent me a long technical email, I could afford to spend however much time it took to understand it.

But many of the people you work with need to keep multiple balls in the air, possibly working under intense pressure against tight deadlines. A colleague in a different department may have opened your two-page email three minutes before a full day of meetings, and, with ten other projects on their plate, may now barely remember what your project is about.

Some functions work toward stable, long-range objectives, while others must respond quickly to urgent, unexpected requests. Some work against critical deadlines, while others have flexibility in almost every deliverable. Some are dependent on social networks to get their jobs done, while others rely on long periods of focused isolation.

The different environments in which we work will impact how we prioritize and manage tasks and how we communicate with other departments during projects. Understanding and respecting these differences will help departments work together without aggravating stress levels or placing demands on others at inappropriate times.

Your Response to These Differences

Understanding these diverse goals, values and working environments will greatly impact how you relate to your colleagues. You'll emphasize results that are important to them. You'll take care to meet the standards that correspond to the values most important to them. And you'll communicate and operate in ways that fit the situation in which they're working—such as understanding the need for concise communication that quickly brings them up to speed on background context and makes any requests or propositions crystal clear.

A Two-Dimensional View of Your Colleagues

Although your colleagues each have their unique personal opinions, goals and values, at work they will tend to have much in common based on where they fall on two axes: the horizontal axis of functional area (e.g., finance, IT, marketing, etc.) and the vertical axis of seniority. Recognizing where people fall on these axes will help you determine how to accomplish your goals and present your progress in ways they appreciate.

Horizontal Axis of Your Organization

Each organization will have several functional areas, such as finance, IT, marketing, human resources, administration, sales, customer service, R&D, the various stages of production and distribution, etc. These functional areas will often be grouped into departments and sometimes deployed within a matrix structure. The reason your colleagues in these departments will tend to be similar is that each function will place specific demands on its employees, and each employee will tend to gravitate to a function matching their personality and skill set.

Some differences between departments will be immediately obvious. (Imagine a group of salespeople and a group of software developers together at a party.) Other differences will be more subtle, but some of these more subtle differences are especially critical to keep in mind as you work with stakeholders and project team members across your organization.

For example, departments often work with their own key performance indicators (KPIs), tracking their progress against these quantifiable measures of how well they're reaching their business goals. Examples would be decreasing the KPI of First Response Time (customer support) or increasing the KPI of Return on Advertising Spend (marketing). Behind such KPIs will be general functional objectives, such as increasing customer satisfaction or making the best use of the marketing budget.

Looking at problems through the lenses of goals, values and working environment can impact how data scientists work with colleagues from other areas. I'll illustrate with three specific functional areas: IT, finance, and marketing.

Information Technology (IT)

You probably have the most in common with your colleagues in IT. In fact, many software developers move to roles as data scientists (and vice versa).

Goals

Your colleagues in IT have two main goals:

1. **Deploy stable code:** Software and systems need to be stable and maintainable and should be developed according to robust procedures that have been developed and refined over many years.

2. **Leverage the best (modern) technology:** There is often a tangible business value in using new techniques and technologies. Advantages may include increased stability, decreased operating cost or greater scalability. Most IT professionals also simply love technology and will naturally want to use newer tools and techniques.

As far as goals are concerned, you definitely share their excitement for new technology. (That may be why you studied machine learning.) You may also feel fairly competent with your programming skills. However, unless you've actually worked in a team of professional software developers, you probably don't truly understand their specific tooling and vocabulary—or the care with which they manage their workflows and quality assurance.

This lack of understanding is going to trip you up as you work with IT. I'll illustrate from my own experience:

> *I once consulted for a company in which the data scientists had built a machine learning tool that promised to significantly improve business results. The data scientists were dependent on IT to deploy the tool. The IT manager, however, took a look at the code and declared that it didn't meet IT standards. The data science manager couldn't appreciate the concerns of the IT manager and wasn't willing to take the time to understand and address his (legitimate) concerns. The disagreement turned into a battle of wills, and the machine learning project died, taking with it all the effort the data scientists had invested.*

It's not without reason that your IT department pushes back heavily when data scientists don't meet their standards for software development. If a production system fails, your IT colleagues are the ones who'll need to fix it at 2:00 a.m. on a Sunday. They're the ones whose career success is partially measured by system stability.

And if a security breach occurs or data is lost because of extra permissions they gave you, no one is going to thank them for being such nice people and bending the rules for you.

Values

IT managers value stable, high-quality code, developed and deployed according to established processes.

Working Environment

IT professionals are typically under a lot of pressure as they try to prioritize and reduce large backlogs and work against long- and short-term deadlines. They generally would like to be left alone to code and dislike being pulled into meetings.

Your Response

Here's my advice for working with IT colleagues:

1. **Understand the development standards in your software teams.** Adhere to them when producing code destined for production. Each team will have standards for unit testing, version control, code checks, documentation, etc.

2. **Be especially friendly to your system admins, IT support and database admins.** These are people you want on your good side! Respect their concerns over access rights. Feel free to make requests and give your reasons, but respect the fact that they need to stick to guidelines.

3. **Keep short lines of communication with IT teams.** Keeping in close touch as you develop projects will help you avoid mistakes that could later hinder deployment of your work.

4. **To the extent possible, use technologies already in use within your company.** This will increase the chance of your project being integrated into existing infrastructure, decrease deployment risk, and generally open the door for more of

your colleagues to understand, contribute to and eventually maintain your project. On a similar note, prefer simpler, more established methods and software packages, unless you can realize a substantial gain from using something more complex.

Before discussing the next functional area, I'll share a personal story related to the second piece of advice above.

> *In one company I worked at, I had, as I usually do, worked hard to develop a positive connection with the guy at the IT help desk. I gave him space when he looked stressed, I made small talk when he was in a better mood, and, when my laptop arrived 10 days late, I didn't complain. I really made an effort to build a positive relationship (which wasn't so hard, as he was a really nice guy when he wasn't overworked).*
>
> *A while later, I happened to need a new laptop. By default, I didn't have admin rights, so this guy asked what software I needed installed. I wrote down all the normal stuff (Slack, Anaconda, etc.), and, as a joke, I added "Fortnite" at the end of the list. Sure enough, Fortnite was there when I picked up the laptop later that day (although the Epic splash screen at system startup was a bit of an embarrassment).*

Finance

Finance departments are critically dependent on accurate, consolidated data. It's quite possible that your finance department was the first sponsor for your organization's data warehousing project and that your data warehouse is still managed from within the finance department (as was the case when I worked at eBay). In this case, it's even more important that you're able to work well with your finance colleagues, as they control much of the data on which you depend.

Finance departments tend to be late adopters of machine learning techniques. As I talk about their goals and values, you'll start to see why.

Goals

In my experience, the two goals of finance that differ most from those of data scientists are precision and timeliness.

1. **Precision:** Numbers need to be precise and should match in every location where they are reported.

2. **Timeliness:** Reports and data need to be available on time. Finance teams are under tremendous pressure to deliver forecasts, budgets and reports at a regular cadence, especially in listed companies.

Values

Finance departments value dependability. Any data or reports required for their ordinary workflow should be rock solid and **on time**. Innovation is icing on the cake, but it should never mix with the cake.

More than anyone else, your colleagues in finance are the ones for whom the decimal points matter, and there's typically **no margin for error**. I'll illustrate with a story:

> *Years ago, a team I was managing was just starting to consolidate mobile traffic data into a new centralized report. The report wasn't finished, but we were making good progress with the data pipeline. I showed the*

> *report to a finance director to update her on our progress. Here was a woman with a giant calculator on her desk. (I'm not making this up.) She could rattle off expense codes by heart.*
>
> *She looked at the prototype report and simply said, "But the numbers don't add up."*
>
> *"Right," I said. "It's not done yet. My point is that we've now got 80% of the data centralized."*
> *But she still didn't get it. Months later, she would still mention the time I had showed her a report where the numbers didn't add up.*
>
> *This director was perhaps a bit of an extreme example, but I did learn my lesson: don't put figures that aren't 100% accurate in front of finance, even if you're trying to make a different point.*

Working Environment

The tasks and workloads of your colleagues in finance will fluctuate, with budget season, quarter-end and year-end being extremely busy. They may need to work weekends to meet critical reporting deadlines. The finance team also frequently gets called into "fire drills," where executives need their support for unexpected but urgent situations.

Your Response

Here's my advice for working with your colleagues in finance:

1. **Clarify exactly what needs to be delivered and by when.**
   This applies whether you're delivering recurring reports or

ad-hoc analysis. Ask them in writing (typically an email) so that it's documented. Clarify terminology if there's any doubt. If you anticipate a problem in meeting their deadline, let them know as soon as possible.

2. **Double- and triple-check any information before you send it.** There are a couple of ways to do this.

   a. Compare values between current and previous reports to detect anomalies.

   b. Compare any partial sums that should match.

3. **When providing reports, prefer tables with exact figures rather than graphs** (more about this in chapter seven). Clearly show dates and data sources on the reports. Also define any ambiguous terminology.

Marketing

Although finance may be the department that launches data warehousing programs, marketing is often the first department to try an innovative data science project. This is partly because marketing tends to have a large discretionary budget and partly because it stands to benefit greatly from what data science has to offer.

Goals

Marketing is hungry for insights into the effectiveness of their investments. They often have millions or even billions of dollars to invest each year, and keeping those budgets depends on demonstrating that they've used the money well. To do this, your marketing colleagues will need to:

1. **Decide how to spend the marketing budget**
   Where should they invest to optimize KPIs such as Return

on Advertising Spend? For example, they'll need to decide which channels to use, who to target, and how much to bid for keywords.

2. **Understand the impact of marketing efforts (attribution)**
It's extremely challenging to understand how the combination of online and offline marketing efforts impacts customer behavior over time in an omni-channel environment.

3. **Establish key partnerships**
Marketers are dependent on certain specialists who produce creative content covering a potentially broad range of themes and mediums, as well as on other specialists who can effectively deliver that content across a diverse advertising ecosystem. Even in the largest companies, internal marketers will typically work with a network of creative and marketing freelancers and agencies who specialize in these different tasks. Identifying the right people and agencies to work with and maintaining a productive working relationship with them are both critical to the success of your marketing colleagues.

Values

Marketing professionals are generally creative, social, free-thinking and very visual. They work in a rapidly changing and highly specialized domain. As such, they will value when you:

1. **Understand marketing techniques and terminology**
The digital marketing landscape is changing very rapidly, so marketers realize they need to work with people who have up-to-date knowledge and skill sets. It's easy to lose credibility with them if they sense you aren't familiar with common tools or terminology.

2. **Create polished visual presentations**

The job of marketers is to produce and deliver compelling images and text, so they naturally look at all presentations with a critical eye in this regard. If you give them analytically robust presentations in a format that's visually unappealing, they're likely to immediately feel a negative reaction to what they're seeing.

I'll illustrate this second point with a personal anecdote:

I once led a team of consultants who were building a cloud-based machine learning tool. Shortly after starting, the team prepared a presentation for the marketing department. A few days after the presentation, I asked the marketing manager if he had any feedback.

After a bit of um-ing and ah-ing, the marketing manager confessed to me that people on his team had remarked that we hadn't incorporated enough color photographs in our presentation! Let me emphasize that our presentation had no practical need for color photographs, but this director was used to seeing random glamour shots of company products in presentations.

I learned my lesson and made sure that all future presentations to his department were visually stunning. The project continued successfully, and we never again received negative feedback related to our presentations.

Working Environment

Marketers are very often either in meetings or preparing for meetings. This is because they need to manage the marketing workflow from budgeting to content creation to campaign execution and eventually to post-campaign reporting and analysis. Each of these stages involves working with completely different subject matter experts, increasing the number of required meetings.

In meetings, marketers work hard to build and protect their professional image, even when the meetings are with contracted third parties. Marketing professionals often change between in-house, agency and freelance work, so it's important for them professionally to maintain their image within the marketing community.

Your Response

Here's my advice for working with marketing colleagues:

1. **Be persistent.** You may find it difficult to schedule time with your marketing colleagues. Be patient but persistent, and try multiple media (scheduled meetings, email, instant messages, or, if all else fails, intercepting them at the coffee machine).

2. **Make an effort to understand their world.** When you do interact, you'll probably hear quite a number of unfamiliar terms and phrases, such as **CPC** versus **CPM**. You'll need to master such terminology or you'll lose credibility with them. On the flip side, realize that they generally won't understand most technical terminology.

3. **Be flexible and responsible.** They're creative, so they may think out loud and frequently change their minds. Accept

this, and don't get annoyed. The positive side of this work style is that they generally will be more flexible in accepting what you provide to them.

4. **Work to see the perspective of the consumer.** This is what marketers do, and practicing it will help you connect with them. Sign up for all of your company's mailing lists. Pause occasionally in your analysis and imagine how your nephew or your grandmother would view the problem or solution.

5. **Make your presentations visually appealing and with a clear message.** Cut out the technical jargon and add a clear takeaway message at the top of each slide.

Summarizing the Horizontal Axis

This discussion of how goals, values and working environments differ between IT, finance and marketing illustrates the importance of approaching colleagues differently according to where they're positioned along the horizontal access of functional areas. What works well with colleagues from one area typically won't work well with colleagues from other areas.

As people move up in level of seniority, their goals, values and working environments tend to change further, eventually coalescing across functional areas to more shared characteristics as they approach board level. In the next section, I'll talk about how these characteristics differ according to level of seniority.

Vertical Axis of Your Organization

Organizations will also have levels of authority and management within and above functional areas, starting with individual contributors (nonmanager) and working up to the level of CEO or president. If you're a recent graduate, you've started as an individual contributor and you're probably interacting with others who are at or just above your level. It can be helpful to understand some of the other vertical segments common in organizations, as they'll have direct impact on your data science projects. I'll start by looking at the top: those who own the organization.

Shareholders

Whether or not your company is publicly listed, one or more people or legal entities own your company and have the ultimate authority. I'll refer to them as the shareholders. The largest shareholders are generally the company founders, large institutional investors (e.g., pension funds), **private equity (PE) firms** or **venture capital (VC) firms**.

Goals

The most common shareholder goal is to increase the value of the company in some way, whether it be a short-term increase in stock price or growth in market share or revenue over a longer horizon. Shareholders may also have environmental or humanitarian goals.

Values

Shareholders value a continual assurance that everything is progressing well with their company, allowing them to focus their energies elsewhere, if they so choose.

Working Environment

The role of the shareholder is in itself passive. Shareholders exercise power by selecting the members of the supervisory board. If they own enough of the company and choose to be actively involved, they can appoint themselves to the supervisory board or even assume an executive role, such as CEO.

Your Response

You won't interact with shareholders unless they also fill one of the subsequent roles.

Supervisory Board (Board of Directors)

I'm going to simplify this slightly, as supervisory boards work differently in different countries. Generally speaking, the members of the supervisory board are individuals who have proven themselves as industry leaders and are paid to supervise the company on a part-time basis. For example, they may be CEOs of other companies or they may work for a VC firm with substantial investment in your company.

Goals

The goals of the supervisory board are to hire the company's CEO, to provide expert advice and to monitor the company's performance.

Values

The supervisory board values being kept informed on how the company is progressing toward its goals.

Working Environment

Members of the supervisory board often have full-time roles at their own companies while maintaining advisory and supervisory roles at several other companies.

Your Response

As far as you and everyone else in your company are concerned, the supervisory board is your most important stakeholder. Your CEO's presentations to the supervisory board must have your highest priority.

C-Suite (Management Team)

The CEO (or president) and their direct reports are generally the most senior full-time (executive) positions in your organization. Note that companies may also give the title of "CxO" to less senior roles. For example, many companies have a Chief Data Officer reporting to the Chief Information Officer, who may in turn report to the CTO or directly to the CEO.

Goals

The CEO leads the other C-level colleagues (CFO, CMO, COO, CTO, etc.) to deliver on the objectives the supervisory board has given them. Although each executive will generally have a function for which they're responsible, they'll work as a team to form corporate strategy and review the progress of the organization across all functions. This gives them both functional—finance, tech, etc.—as well as organizational—strategy, **mergers and acquisitions (M&A)**, etc.—responsibilities.

The C-suite members may not have subject matter expertise in the way that we'd think of expertise. Their goals are both to decide on high-level issues—organization, strategy, and budgeting—and to hire and manage talented people who can themselves oversee the work within their respective functional areas.

Values

Members of the C-suite are reliant on their staff to deliver on their objectives and to keep the organization running smoothly. This being the case, they value delivery on objectives, strong communication skills, leadership and the ability to work well within the internal organization that the company leadership has constructed.

Working Environment

Because C-level employees constitute the executive leadership team of your organization, they'll participate together in planning and reporting meetings spanning a wide range of topics, giving them a very broad view of the company but limiting the time they can invest in understanding the operational details of their own areas. They may also be drawn into external activities, such as M&A, placing further demands on their time.

In the time they have left for their own functional areas, they'll need to provide top-level visionary leadership and hire strong staff they can trust with project execution.

Your Response

If you're an individual contributor, it's difficult to understand the true priorities and concerns of the C-suite beyond what you read in company memos. You may be excited about moving your company forward in the use of AI, but understand that this is generally not a top priority of the C-suite, unless it aligns with the priorities coming to them from the supervisory board. You should generally frame any reports you're working on for the C-suite in terms of company-level goals and KPIs.

Senior and Executive Management

Between the C-suite and your direct (line) manager, there may be several layers of management. The more senior they are, the more responsibilities they'll have and the more balls they'll need to keep in the air simultaneously. This translates to less time for project details.

Goals

Senior managers' success hinges on hiring and incentivizing staff. They also need to effectively communicate in multiple directions, both horizontally and vertically.

Their broad range of responsibilities forces them to delegate responsibility, which in turn puts them in the precarious position of being responsible for results while depending on others to deliver those results.

Being in this difficult situation, senior managers need to identify individuals they can rely on to deliver results and advisors they can trust to provide accurate insights and recommendations. These trusted advisors serve as "gatekeepers" for the senior manager.

Values

Senior managers value people who can take ownership for projects and subject matter areas, communicate clearly, and successfully navigate interdepartmental relations. I'll cover these first two skills in particular in chapters six through nine.

Working Environment

It's important to realize that senior managers typically won't understand technical details and, because they're responsible for so many projects, they need to switch gears frequently and rapidly. They need to very quickly process the massive amounts of information they receive, understanding what is and is not important. This is all the harder for them as they'll be receiving a mixture of high- and low-level details, much of which they won't understand, often from people who haven't yet developed the skill to communicate clearly and concisely.

Your Response

Because senior managers need to quickly scan correspondence for the most important points, your communication with them needs to be concise, clear and easily scannable. It should include clear subject lines and highlighted requests and conclusions. Use the principles of visual hierarchy I'll present in chapter seven. Also, keep your technical terminology to a minimum, realizing that they're now several steps removed from that level of detail.

Work through their gatekeepers where possible, such as their immediate reports or colleagues with whom they often interact. The gatekeepers will generally be more accessible, have more time to hear you out, and be in a better position to influence the ultimate decision makers.

The extent to which it may be appropriate for you to work with senior managers depends on the cultural dimension of power distance, which I'll talk about in chapter three.

Line Management

Directly above you in the organizational chart is your line manager, the person to whom you report. Your line manager may understand the details of your work and may also be doing hands-on work.

Goals

Even if they're doing work similar to yours, the goals of your line manager are generally much different from your goals as an individual contributor. Your line manager needs to define and deliver on team-level goals, keeping their own manager happy while also managing a diverse team under them. They need to collaborate with managers of other teams, some of whom will be actively competing with them for resources and/or the possibility of future promotion.

If this is your first job out of school, it's quite possible that your line manager is also in their first management role, so they'll be learning how to be a manager at the same time you're adjusting to having a manager.

Values

As with more senior management, your line manager will generally place value on you taking ownership for projects. (I'll talk more in chapter nine about what "taking ownership" means.) More than anyone else, your line manager will also place heavy value on your meeting the goals and standards that they set for you, sometimes given in the form of your annual targets but more often in the direct day-to-day feedback they give you.

Working Environment

Your line manager needs to manage multiple lines of communication, coordinate projects between teams, and deliver on several projects centered around a common theme. This gives them more insight into the big picture, which you can benefit from, but it also means they need to balance what's important to you with what's important to others around them. They'll have less time to go into technical details and will feel more pressure to make timely decisions.

Your Response

You'll help your manager by taking complete responsibility for the tasks you do, communicating clearly and frequently, and being highly responsive to their requests, priorities, and ways of working. I'll talk more about how to do this in chapters eight and nine.

Remember that your line manager is your ultimate gatekeeper. Other managers will rely on their evaluation of you, so if your line manager doesn't approve of your work, there's not much use trying to prove yourself to anyone else in the company. Going behind their back is generally a recipe for disaster. If you really don't respect them, keep your opinion to yourself and look for a position within a different team or company.

> *I've had about a dozen line managers over the course of my career. Some were data scientists; others weren't. A few didn't seem to take the role seriously, others tried their best, two were at some point fired on the spot by their own managers, and one was what I would consider a "good manager."*

Your manager needs to know that you're responding to their input. If they give you negative feedback, make sure you understand what they mean and what they expect in the future. Accept the feedback and make it clear to them that you understand what they're saying. We tend to want to defend our actions to make ourselves look better, but this is generally not the right approach with our managers.

> *A person who once reported to me, on the rare occasion when I gave him negative feedback, would always first listen to me and then end the discussion with, "OK, I understand." This reassured me, as his manager, that my concerns were understood, that the problem was resolved and that we could forget the matter and move on. If he had instead started with*

excuses, then I'd have worried that the problem would reoccur. (There were also rare occasions when my criticism was based on a complete misunderstanding, in which case, of course, he cleared up the misunderstanding.)

Summarizing the Vertical Axis

If and when you do have the opportunity to interact with more senior levels of your organization, it's important that you be aware of the pressures and priorities that they're working with. In particular, craft a clear message that concisely communicates the background, your progress and your key conclusions and requests. Frame this in terms of the goals and values of your senior audience, depending on their position on the vertical axis. The gatekeepers around you, your line manager in particular, are typically the best ones to help you prepare this presentation. In chapter six, I'll elaborate on techniques for crafting a concise message.

In Conclusion

It is indeed challenging, but critical, for you, as a data scientist, to understand the diverse landscape around you. As you make the effort to adjust to the goals, values and work environments of your colleagues within different departments, and your seniors at different levels of the company, you'll begin to understand how to relate in ways that increase their trust in you and open the door for you to deliver value for them.

This chapter introduced basic principles that will help you start to produce value in your organization. I'll continue with this topic later, in section four, when I discuss leading projects and constructing road maps. But before I start on those more advanced topics, I'll first cover three subjects crucial for relating with your colleagues. The first of these subjects focuses on the subtle or not-so-subtle cultural differences you'll encounter within organizations.

Additional Reading

Goldsmith, M., & Reiter, M. (2007). *What got you here won't get you there: How successful people become even more successful.* Hyperion.

Tusa, J. (2020). *On board: The insider's guide to surviving life in the boardroom.* Bloomsbury Business.

TOPIC TWO

• • • •

Colleagues

CHAPTER THREE

Thriving in a Workplace with Diverse Cultures

Although each culture in this world is unique, as individuals we generally start life assuming everyone shares our core values. We personally define what is "normal" behavior. Eventually, we interact with people from different backgrounds, and we're forced to reconsider our assumptions.

As data scientists, you'll almost certainly work closely with colleagues from other cultures. If both you and they don't recognize and respect the fundamental differences between your cultures, it won't be long before you misunderstand a particular statement or action in some very significant way.

Cultural misunderstandings are especially dangerous when they relate to deep-seated values, leading you to misjudge the other person's core character. Within an organization, you'll certainly need to understand and accommodate cultural differences, as they'll otherwise limit your ability to work together.

In nearly every company for which I've worked, the data science teams were composed of people from diverse cultures. In my leadership role at eBay, I was an American based in Amsterdam, managing a team in China and collaborating regularly with teams spread across six continents.

Here's what I learned: Although sometimes difficult to pinpoint, differences between cultures can have a huge impact on teamwork and workflow in data science projects. Even in our technical work, it's critical to our business success to be aware of the cultural undercurrents that can cause misunderstandings and major conflict.

Here's an example from my own experience to illustrate.

> *The team in one of my first jobs after university consisted of people from a mixture of cultures, including colleagues born and raised in various Asian countries. During one team meeting, I frankly stated that our coding standards should be higher. No one replied, but a few weeks later, my Asian manager told me privately that my comment was not appropriate in a group setting. I came to understand his perspective more clearly throughout the following months, as I observed how all feedback from the Asian team members was passed anonymously through the team manager.*

In the Netherlands, where I've spent the past decade, people tend to be extremely direct, whereas the English across the channel are the exact opposite, communicating with subtle nuances designed to mask their underlying thoughts. I've seen colleagues from these two countries drive each other crazy as they try to communicate about progress, plans and commitments.

A similar disparity exists between the French and the Germans. A French colleague once confessed how he would often ignore emails in which his manager wasn't cc'd. My German colleague, on hearing this, responded that she would be extremely offended if someone cc'd her manager on an email.

Or consider working hours. If it's five in the afternoon, a Dutch father will pack up and leave work to pick up his child from daycare. In countries such as Portugal, the father will stay at the office until his manager leaves, even if it means sitting at his desk watching YouTube. If it's noon, a French colleague leaves for a two-hour lunch, infuriating his Dutch colleagues, who have quickly downed light sandwiches with a glass of buttermilk, returning to their desks by 12:30. I've actually sat in meetings with Dutch data scientists as they've complained to me about this exact situation.

Understanding cultural differences can help guide day-to-day interaction, and it can help us choose the appropriate response to awkward situations.

I recently needed to decline an invitation to an event organized by a Middle Eastern woman because the event conflicted with my daughter's birthday. I declined up front and gave the excuse that I had "a prior commitment." This was an appropriate response according to my American background, in which companies often expect you to put work above family. However, a colleague of mine who had worked closely with this woman and who was more familiar with her culture told me in private that I should have instead explained to her that it was my daughter's birthday, as family was given high priority in her culture. In fact, many cultures expect you to always initially accept such an invitation, regardless of whether you plan to attend, and then simply cancel at the last moment.

Introduction of the Hofstede Cultural Dimensions

I could list hundreds of such specific cultural nuances, each of which has the potential to trip you up when working with colleagues from different cultures. Rather than writing such an impossibly exhaustive list, I'd like to present one particular framework for thinking of how cultures differ.

The framework I'll present in this chapter was developed by social psychologist Gerard Hofstede. Although the research underpinning it began in the 1970s, the model has been continually refined in the decades since, with the final dimension published in 2010. The model that Hofstede progressively developed eventually encompassed six dimensions, each of which describes a fundamental way cultures differ in their norms and values. These fundamental differences manifest themselves in particular characteristics—the cultural differences that may surprise us in our colleagues, such as taking two-hour lunch breaks, talking back to managers, or staying late at the office even when there's no work left to do.

These are the six dimensions:

1. **Power Distance:** Do we expect power to be distributed unequally?

2. **Uncertainty Avoidance:** Are we comfortable with unstructured situations?

3. **Individualism:** Is our identity drawn from the community around us?

4. **Gender Difference:** Should men and women have different fundamental characteristics and values, or should there be little difference?

5. **(Long-Term) Pragmatic:** Do we focus on a long- or short-term time horizon, and how does this focus impact our adherence to values and principles?

6. **Indulgence:** Should we focus on enjoying life or on fulfilling responsibilities?

I'll include some country ratings in the discussions below, as illustrations, but I do want to stress that the increased flow of people and information across national borders over the past few decades has blurred cultural differences that were more distinct when Hofstede started his research several decades ago. And yet cultural differences persist, especially those deeply ingrained in us from an early age.

Now let's take a closer look at each of the six dimensions and how they may impact your work as a data scientist. I'll start the discussion of each dimension by asking your reaction to specific work situations that I've encountered myself. Your responses will depend on your culture. I'll then describe the dimension in question, listing countries at the extreme ends of the scale and giving examples of how each extreme could impact a data science team. I'll end each section with tips for dealing with colleagues who differ from you with respect to that dimension.

Power Distance

Ask yourself the following questions:

> *After running into your manager's manager and having a brief discussion, you want to send him an idea by email. Is that OK?*

> *Assume you have a great idea that needs support from another team. Do you need to convince the individuals on that team, or only the team's manager?*

All cultures are unequal to some degree, but some are more unequal than others.

In lower power distance (PD) cultures, the hierarchy is established for convenience but doesn't imply existential value. Senior leaders should be approachable and enjoy no more respect than anyone else. Subordinates expect to be consulted and will object if they're not or if they don't agree with a decision. Everyone expects power to be used legitimately and to be subject to objective governance. Corruption is rare and will generally lead to removal from office. Organizations tend to be flatter, with more delegated authority.

In high PD cultures, positions of power are considered to be fundamental aspects of society, whether the leaders are good or bad. Seniority implies existential superiority, and leaders should be obeyed regardless. It's considered normal that leaders are paid more and have more privileges. High PD typically results in complex, centralized organizations in which decisions are delayed to consult higher-ups.

Figure 4 shows countries with some of the highest and lowest power distance scores. Links to data sources for this and subsequent charts are in the footnote.[7]

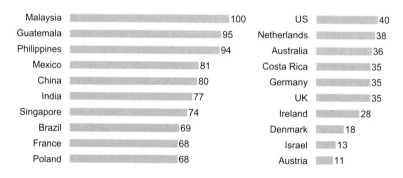

Figure 4. Countries with highest and lowest power distance

---

[7] Values shown in this chapter are from https://www.hofstede-insights.com/, http://clearlycultural.com/, https://geerthofstede.com/wp-content/uploads/2016/08/ Indulgence-vs-Restraint-in-10-minutes-2015-09-05.pptx and https://geerthofstede.com/wp-content/uploads/2016/08/Long-Short-Term-Orientation-in-10-minutes-2015-09-05.pptx, as referenced in August 2020.

Returning to the two questions at the beginning of this section, in a high PD company, you wouldn't send the email to your manager's manager. Doing so would risk upsetting your manager, who might feel that their position of authority was being undermined. And to get support from another team in a high PD culture, you could focus on convincing the manager, who would in turn dictate their decision to the team. In a low PD culture, you would also need to convince the individual team members.

Tips for working with differing levels of Power Distance

1. Any leader in your company from a high PD culture will expect their status to be acknowledged. They may even be accustomed to being called "boss." This person will generally expect to be followed with little pushback, so don't openly challenge their authority. Voice your disagreement carefully.

2. Team members from high PD cultures will want to consult their managers before making decisions, so don't expect immediate responses from them. If you're the manager of a high PD employee, don't be surprised if your direct report seems to always be waiting for you to make decisions or take initiative. Continue to reassure this person that you trust them to make decisions. If and when they make mistakes, give them positive feedback for taking the risk to act independently.

3. If you want support from high PD colleagues, go through their managers first. If you want support from low PD colleagues, you'll need to convince them directly. However, if their manager is high PD, you'll need to speak first with the manager, or else you'll get resistance from the resentful manager later.

Although power distance is perhaps the most intuitively clear of the six dimensions, the next dimension I'll discuss has perhaps the greatest impact on data science projects.

Uncertainty Avoidance

Ask yourself the following questions:

How comfortable are you being assigned a project with no clear structure or milestones?

Do you expect your manager to continually check up on your work and provide input, or rather to give you a lot of space to work by yourself?

Let me start by clarifying that uncertainty avoidance (UA) is not the same as risk avoidance. It is, rather, the degree to which cultures are comfortable with unstructured situations or situations that are in some way novel or unusual.

Cultures with high UA will try to minimize the odds of facing such situations by establishing strict behavioral codes, laws and rules. There's a story that when the European Union was first established, member countries who were high UA pushed for more rules and regulations. Cynics said these countries were not planning to hold to the new rules but simply wanted everything to be clear and unambiguous.

In high UA cultures, teachers are expected to have answers for everything; knowledge systems should contain ultimate truths. High UA cultures may be less tolerant of deviant ideas, considering them to be dangerous. Individuals are less likely to change jobs, but the heightened need for control tends to cause more work-related stress.

In contrast, individuals from low UA cultures view uncertainty as natural. They'll generally take each day as it comes, will readily admit if they don't have an answer, and generally feel less stress at work. Low

UA cultures dislike excessive rules, whether written or unwritten. Their workers change jobs more readily.

Figure 5 shows some of the countries with the highest and lowest uncertainty avoidance scores.

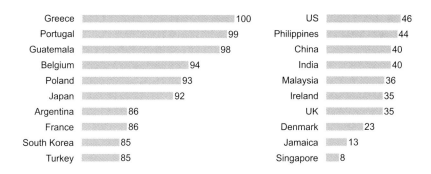

Figure 5. Countries with highest and lowest uncertainty avoidance

Returning to the two questions at the beginning of this section, if you're from a high UA culture, you generally won't be comfortable if you aren't given some clear structure in your projects, including regular input from your manager. If you're from a low UA culture, you'll enjoy the freedom to find your own way and will probably resent too much input from your manager.

Misunderstandings based on uncertainty avoidance hit teams especially hard in Europe, as European countries span the range from most to least avoidant of uncertainty. And while the symptoms of uncertainty avoidance are obvious, the fact that these symptoms are cultural, rather than individual, is not obvious.

For example, a manager from a low UA culture (e.g., Denmark) may assign a task to a data scientist from a high UA culture (e.g., Greece) and give very little instruction or guidance. While the Dane believes they're being a good manager by keeping distance, the Greek, feeling extremely uncomfortable with the lack of guidance, may simply wait for more instruction before starting the task. On the flip side, a Greek manager may feel that they need to provide very detailed instructions and guidelines to a Danish data scientist, who in turn will feel smothered and micromanaged.

Tips for working with differing levels of Uncertainty Avoidance

When working with high UA colleagues:

1. Be clear about your goals, parameters, and expectations. Make it a point to communicate more than you typically would. Give them the opportunity to asks questions, and don't take it personally if they seem frustrated or critical of the lack of detail you initially provide.

2. Be aware that there may be unspoken cultural rules and expectations you'll need to learn. Again, as you increase communication with them and work to understand what they say, you'll grow aware of what these rules and expectations may be. If you're working in their cultural environment, you should also ask for the opinion of others not involved in the conflict. These third parties can help illuminate the unspoken elements you may have missed.

When working with low UA colleagues:

1. Don't create too much structure (but do ensure people stay focused). As you assign tasks, focus on high-level goals and give individuals freedom in how they reach those goals. This may cause you stress, but reassure yourself by asking them to describe their thought processes and the actions they've taken toward reaching the specified goals.

2. Don't come across as knowing all the answers. Understand that your low UA colleagues need freedom to explore ideas themselves. Choose which issues and assumptions are most critical to assert, and have some flexibility with the others. For example, you may insist that the model targets a particular metric, but hold your tongue when your team member's presentation slide includes a design element you don't particularly like.

I mentioned that uncertainty avoidance has a large impact on data scientists. The reason is that data science projects are by nature highly uncertain. We're uncertain about data, model fit, deployment, model decay, stakeholder buy-in, compliance, etc. Not only data scientists, but also their stakeholders, need to be able to tolerate high levels of uncertainty.

I experienced this myself when I was helping a company set up a new data science program, and the manager of the business intelligence team was from a high UA culture. Every few months, he would get very stressed that the data science program was developing too quickly, and he would complain that he didn't have enough oversight into what was going on. In this case, my primary stakeholder, a senior executive at the company, had low uncertainty avoidance, so we were able to reassure that manager and continue our rapid project development.

Individualism vs. Collectivism

Ask yourself the following questions:

> *You're in a team meeting and think your colleague is doing something wrong. Do you frankly vocalize your criticism?*

> *Your new colleagues invite you to join them for lunch, but you have a lot of work to do. What should you tell them?*

In this dimension, we measure the degree to which people in a society integrate into groups and the extent to which they're expected to show loyalty to communities beyond their core families.

Collective cultures naturally form cohesive groups that provide protection to their members in exchange for loyalty. This sense of belonging is very important, so there's a natural formation of "in" and "out" groups. Relationships are more important than tasks or even moral norms, and members avoid criticizing other group members. Thus, emotions are generally suppressed in the interest of harmony.

Individualistic cultures, on the other hand, expect people to care for themselves and to have the right to privacy and time alone. Individual opinion is valued, and speaking one's mind is considered a good thing. Tasks prevail over relationships.

> *For several years, I managed a team of Chinese developers based in Shanghai, while I myself was working in Amsterdam. I was amazed at the cohesion within the Shanghai team. Not only would they spend long days working together, they would often spend large portions of the weekend hanging out, sometimes singing karaoke until early hours of Saturday morning. (It shouldn't have come as a surprise when two team members eventually married.)*

At the same time, I noticed a subtle difference in how the Chinese communicated about their colleagues. Part of my standard interview questionnaire was to ask applicants to describe a person from their past whom they had enjoyed working with and another person whom they had not enjoyed working with. I noticed that few if any of the Chinese applicants were willing to describe a former colleague in negative terms. I soon dropped this question for Chinese applicants.

Figure 6 shows countries with some of the highest and lowest scores for individualism.

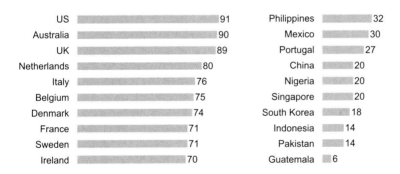

US	91	Philippines	32
Australia	90	Mexico	30
UK	89	Portugal	27
Netherlands	80	China	20
Italy	76	Nigeria	20
Belgium	75	Singapore	20
Denmark	74	South Korea	18
France	71	Indonesia	14
Sweden	71	Pakistan	14
Ireland	70	Guatemala	6

Figure 6. Countries with highest and lowest individualism

Returning to the two questions at the beginning of this section, if you are in a collective culture, you should be extra careful not to say something that would make a colleague look bad in a group setting. You will want to participate in group social events, such as joining your team for lunch, whenever possible. Both of these are less critical (albeit still valued) practices within individualistic cultures.

Tips for working with differing levels of Individualism

When working with individualistic colleagues:

1. Acknowledge their individual accomplishments. They generally will appreciate feeling that they're exceptional in some way.

2. Realize that they may choose not to mix work and social life. They may be friendly and even talk about their personal lives while at work, but don't be offended if they don't join you for drinks or dinner afterward.

3. Encourage debate and expression of individual ideas. They'll grow frustrated if they feel they're not allowed to express their opinions.

When working with collectivist colleagues:

1. Try to spend time together while you're not working, such as during meals or social events. You may find they even appreciate being asked to do things together on weekends.

2. Avoid expressing negative feelings or expressing negativity toward the ideas of others, particularly in public. These cultures use other channels for feedback—channels that are acceptable in their respective cultures but that may seem unusual to you. Find out what those channels are for the cultures you interact with.

3. Highlight group, rather than individual, accomplishments. Celebrating team accomplishments with team social events works well, as these cultures are more open to having such events outside of working hours.

Since a sense of affiliation is such a core human need, we can see how cultural misunderstandings in this dimension can cause deep emotional turmoil and potentially lead to serious conflict. The stark difference in voicing of opinions and criticism between individualistic and collective cultures can also easily short-circuit your team projects if not handled wisely.

Gender Difference

Ask yourself the following questions:

> *Is it reasonable to expect employees to stay at work until seven in the evening?*
>
> *Should you motivate your team by appealing to their egos or to their sense of comradery?*

Hofstede's next dimension focuses on the degree to which a society believes that the roles and values of men should differ from the roles and values of women. Although he called this dimension "masculinity," I feel that the term "gender difference" is a better descriptor, and that's the term I'll use throughout this chapter.

In high gender difference cultures, men are expected to be more assertive and ambitious, putting work before family and generally focusing on facts and actions rather than emotions and feelings. Egos tend to run strong, and money and achievement are common measures of success.

In low gender difference cultures, however, there's little psychological differentiation between genders and little differentiation in their social roles. Men are expected to balance work and family, show empathy, and prefer consensus over competition. There is more focus on quality of life than on gains in finance or status.

These cultural differences play out in a number of ways at work. If an employer assumes an employee will stay at work until seven every evening, they're implicitly assuming that someone else is at home to take care of the children. If the focus is on achieving competitive KPIs, they're assuming that teams are motivated by ego, competition and a desire to win.

A Danish friend once described to me what happened when an American took over as CEO of his company. The American (high gender difference) tried to motivate the Danes (low gender difference) with competitive metrics and pressured them to stay longer at work rather than join their families for dinner. (Note: Danes generally catch up on work in the evening.) The result was internal rebellion, leading even to corporate sabotage. It was a complete cultural mismatch.

Figure 7 shows countries with high and low gender difference scores.

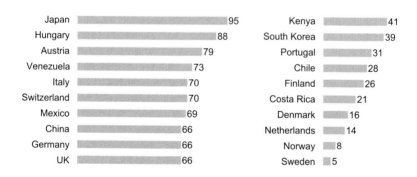

Figure 7. Countries with highest and lowest gender difference

Returning to the two questions at the beginning of this section, cultures with low gender difference scores would not expect employees to work late at the office, as they acknowledge that all employees with children, men or women, will occasionally need to pick their kids up from daycare.

For the second question, appealing to ego works best with high gender difference cultures but may be counterproductive with low gender difference cultures.

Tips for working with differing perspectives on Gender Difference

When working with high gender difference cultures:

1. If you feel your colleague holds strong prejudices related to gender, understand that they may be prevalent in that culture, not only in that person.

2. Be prepared for the expectation that you will work long hours and generally put work above family.

3. When working to motivate your colleagues, try to set precise targets and appeal to egos and bragging rights.

When working with low gender difference cultures:

1. Focus on the processes of negotiation and collaboration rather than highlighting ways you're competing with associates.

2. Respect that your colleagues need to balance work and family responsibilities. Provide them flexibility to work outside of regular hours when necessary.

Some elements of the dimension of gender difference will be immediately apparent to you, while others become more noticeable as you grow in seniority and as your family responsibilities increase.

These first four cultural dimensions were the original ones that Hofstede developed. He later added the next two: (long-term) pragmatic and indulgence. I'll cover them only briefly, as they're more abstract and perhaps a bit less relevant to your work.

(Long-Term) Pragmatic

Ask yourself the following questions:

Is compromise a sign of strength or of weakness?

Do I gain or lose respect by selling myself strongly?

Broadly speaking, this dimension focuses on the time horizon the society orients itself toward—long-term or short-term—as well as the implications this orientation has on how pragmatic the culture is.

Cultures oriented toward the long-term generally perceive individuals as playing only a small role within a much larger story. This perspective promotes personal modesty as well as attention to thrift and education. Such cultures are generally more willing to bend rules in favor of "swimming with the current," and thus tend to operate pragmatically.

Cultures with a short-term orientation, on the other hand, expect individuals to take action in support of core principles and values, even if it means swimming against the current now or potentially placing the future at risk. Individuals are expected to justify their actions against a set of norms, which leads to a culture where people tend to promote their own achievements.

Figure 8 shows some of the most (long-term) pragmatic and (short-term) normative countries. (Higher values are more long-term oriented.)

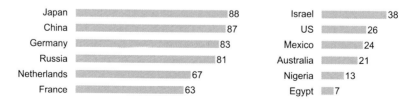

Figure 8. (Long-term) pragmatic vs. (short-term) normative countries

Returning to the two questions at the beginning of this section, a (short-term) normative culture will see compromise as a sign of weakness rather than wisdom, while a (long-term) pragmatic culture will view people who sell themselves strongly as arrogant.

Tips for working with differing levels of (Long-Term) Pragmatic

When working with colleagues from (long-term) pragmatic cultures:

1. Behave modestly. Don't talk too much about yourself.

2. Communicate in the language of compromises, as they're more likely to see compromise as a good thing.

3. Recognize that people may be willing to bend established rules to accommodate the peculiarities of a specific situation.

When working with colleagues from (short-term) normative cultures:

1. Sell yourself strongly.

2. Understand that people may lose respect for you if you seem willing to compromise principles that they feel are inviolable.

Note how many Asian and European countries score high in (long-term) pragmatic, in strong contrast to countries such as the US and Australia.

Indulgence

Ask yourself the following questions:

Is it a good idea to make jokes during a business meeting?

How important is work-life balance?

Indulgence quantifies the preference for personal gratification over fulfillment of duty. It impacts attitudes toward freedom of speech, involvement in sports, adherence to moral codes, and even levels of obesity.

Employees from indulgent cultures make career choices based on personal fulfillment, development opportunities, and work-life balance. Low indulgence cultures view work as an obligation and a responsibility to be taken very seriously. For example, a customer service representative in an indulgent culture would be expected to smile, while one in a restrained culture might consider smiling inappropriate for their professional role.

I once tried to recruit a candidate from a low indulgence culture by appealing to work-life balance. He declined the job, saying he didn't mind heavy workloads.

Figure 9 shows countries with the highest and lowest levels of indulgence.

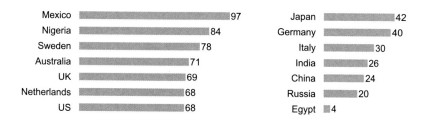

Figure 9. Countries with highest and lowest indulgence

Returning to the two questions at the beginning of this section, high indulgence cultures would appreciate light jokes in a business environment, and they would value work-life balance.

Tips for working with differing levels of Indulgence

When working with colleagues from indulgent cultures:

1. Try to have fun at work and help your colleagues enjoy themselves. Make jokes and laugh with your colleagues. If you see something funny online, share it (but not so often that it seems you're not working). Some people even bring food to share.

2. If you're a manager, actively work with your staff to create personal development plans, including coaching and mentoring, so that they see themselves as benefiting from their current role.

3. Encourage debate and dialogue during meetings so that everyone feels they're valued.

4. If you have the authority, give your staff more options for balancing work and recreation, such as working from home or taking unpaid sabbaticals.

When working with colleagues from restrained cultures:

1. Be professional while at work. Your colleagues may not feel that a relaxed attitude is appropriate in the work environment.

2. Think about your personal goals, such as work-life balance or personal development, and take responsibility for achieving them. But don't expect that your employer will help you with them or even appreciate it if you mention that these are your goals.

In Conclusion

The Hofstede Dimensions give us a starting point when trying to understand underlying cultural mindsets that may be influencing our colleagues. More than anything, learning about them is a foundation from which to grow our awareness of the myriad cultural nuances that may impact our work.

Be mindful that each culture, in fact each *individual*, is unique. Be sensitive to differences and do all you can to earn trust and good-will at the start of your relationships with colleagues, so when misunderstandings do arise (as they surely will), you'll have a strong basis from which to work through them.

If you'd like to compare your country's culture with that of one or more colleagues, you can use the online tool at https://www.hofstede-insights.com/product/compare-countries/. As an example, here is how the US (my country of origin), the Netherlands (my current home) and China (where my data warehouse team was based) compare:

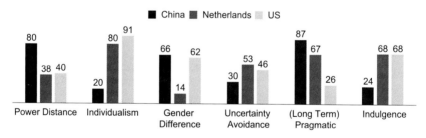

Figure 10. Comparison of China, US and NL

Cultural differences can be subtle and confusing, but once you understand them, they're in some sense an easier type of conflict to deal with than others. In the next two chapters, I'll talk about progressively more difficult interpersonal challenges. Chapter four will discuss reaching agreement, and chapter five will discuss office politics, or conflicts that arise when objectives and judgments are generally not transparent.

Additional Reading

Hofstede, G., Hofstede, G. J., & Minkov, M. (2010). *Cultures and organizations: Software of the mind* (3rd ed.). McGraw-Hill Professional.

Meyer, E. (2014). T*he culture map: Breaking through the invisible boundaries of global business.* PublicAffairs.

Morrison, T., & Conaway, W. A. (2006). *Kiss, bow, or shake hands: The bestselling guide to doing business in more than 60 countries.* Adams Media.

The Mind Tools website, https://www.mindtools.com/pages/article/newLDR_66.htm, also includes some good examples and business tips related to the Hofstede model.

CHAPTER FOUR

Reaching Agreement

What was the most recent negotiation you had at work? Or is there something you'd like to negotiate for in the near future? When I ask younger data scientists what they'd like help in negotiating, they almost always say salary. The more experienced would say negotiating project scope or the tooling available to them. Personally, I often find myself trying to convince other departments to support one of my projects in some way, such as by providing access to their data.

This chapter focuses on the situation where **both sides** recognize that there's some disagreement or conflict, perhaps in opinions or objectives. This mutual recognition of the problem is a great starting point for conflict resolution—a starting point we didn't have when I discussed cultural differences (chapter three) and again won't have when I discuss office politics (chapter five).

I won't talk here about how to win arguments, and I won't even talk about how to reach a compromise. Rather, I'll talk about techniques for clearing obstacles in negotiations—obstacles that might otherwise prevent you from identifying mutually beneficial solutions. Along the way, I'll give some examples from my own experience.

The first obstacle is that we often don't actually realize the true causes behind our disagreements. We've found ourselves in a discussion about salary, priorities, or permissions, but those topics are only part of the challenge we face in reaching agreement. The other part, the personal dimension, often lies unrecognized or unspoken.

And yet, it's only by first addressing the personal dimension that we'll be able to effectively address the issue we set out to negotiate.

Start by Focusing on the Personal Dimension

We each bring our core motivations, perspectives and emotions to every negotiation. However, you almost certainly don't understand what your counterpart is thinking or feeling at the first moment of disagreement. Very likely, you don't even fully understand what you yourself are thinking or feeling. To have an effective negotiation, you'll first need to understand yourself and your position fully. I'll illustrate this briefly by looking at motivations, perspectives and emotions— yours and your counterparts'.

Motivations

Let's start with what's motivating you to take your particular position in the negotiation. What's driving you may not be what you think. To keep it simple, let's continue with the example of salary negotiations.

When junior data scientists talk with me about negotiating their salaries, it's easy for them to get stuck on a number, especially after they've compared salaries with friends.

But when I ask them to explain to me why they want a salary increase, I find they seldom have a serious need for the money. Their real motivation is one or more of the following:

1. *A higher salary makes them feel more valued.*
2. *They feel they aren't being treated fairly.*
3. *They want their company to acknowledge their performance.*
4. *They want to see their career progress.*

Although these data scientists say they want a higher salary, the reality is that something deeper is motivating them—something that they perhaps haven't yet clarified in their own thinking.

If we don't even clearly understand what's motivating us, we certainly won't understand what's motivating the other person. So think carefully about what may be motivating you, and work hard to understand the motivations of your counterpart. You'll come to better understand their position through active listening and, as appropriate, direct questions. I'll talk more about this process later in the chapter.

Perspectives

Your perspective on the negotiation is unique to your situation. In fact, your perspective may be drastically different from that of your counterpart. You're thinking of how your salary is lower than that of friends in comparable roles at other companies. Your manager, however, is remembering the hard internal battle they fought to give you a starting salary above the top of your salary band. They may also be considering how you don't yet take as much responsibility as others in your team.

We seldom vocalize our perspectives, and yet they play a crucial role in how we choose to negotiate. Again, this is true for both of you. As another example, consider the permissions on your computer.

A common challenge for you as a data scientist is to get admin rights on your company laptop. You know why you want the admin access (to update software libraries, install IDEs, etc.), but what is the perspective of the system administrator? The sys admin deals mostly with colleagues who neither need nor understand the dangers of admin rights. The sys admin carries a heavy responsibility for network security, including guarding against ransomware and loss of confidential information. Their perception of admin rights is very different from yours.

We may never fully understand each other's perceptions related to the issue at hand, but, as with motivations, we must start out by recognizing that each of our perceptions are unique and then do what we can to understand them.

Your perceptions will be closely connected with the third, and most powerful, personal element of negotiations: emotions.

Emotions

Emotions have more of an influence on your conflicts than you may realize. Strong emotions can completely dominate and often derail any negotiation, regardless of the substance. For this reason, it's critical to understand the emotions of the other person, as well as your own.

Yes, as with motivations, it's important to be aware of your own emotions. During negotiations, are you getting tense? Angry? Nervous? If so, ask yourself why. If emotions are spilling over from other areas of your life (such as problems at home), be conscious that you don't allow that anger or negativity to influence unrelated negotiations at work.

If either side of the negotiation is responding with strong emotion, it could be a sign that a core human interest is being threatened. In their classic bestseller *Getting to Yes*,[8] authors Fisher and Ury list five such core interests that, when threatened, will stir strong emotional responses:

1. **Autonomy:** Is someone losing the ability to make their own decisions and steer their own path? Autonomy is easily threatened during conflict.

---

[8] Fisher, R., Ury, W. L., & Patton, B. (2011). *Getting to yes: Negotiating agreement without giving in* (3rd rev. ed.). Penguin Books.

2. **Appreciation:** Is someone's job being undervalued? Do they perceive that others aren't utilizing the results of their work?

3. **Affiliation:** Acceptance in a peer group. Does someone feel their membership in the team is being threatened? Do they feel bypassed?

4. **Role:** Having a meaningful purpose. Do our colleagues in corporate governance (sys admins, privacy officers, etc.) feel we don't respect their roles?

5. **Status:** Acknowledgement of the respect due their position. If a person feels they should have been consulted or involved in the process earlier, they'll perceive this failure as an affront to their perceived status.

When you encounter strong resistance that seems to come out of nowhere, think about whether one of these five core interests may be involved. I'll illustrate with an example.

> I worked with an executive who was given ownership of an organization's data warehouse along with management of the central team of data scientists. A different department decided to launch independent data science projects and use a separate cloud provider for their data storage. At one point, they asked the first executive if he could share a data source with them, but the executive refused to share any of the data under his control. This turned out to be an extremely difficult disagreement to negotiate because the underlying issue was not the data, but, rather, that the executive had perceived this new project as a challenge to his status as internal owner of the data and data science projects.

Before proceeding with the next section, take another moment to read through the five core values above. Think for a moment about whether you feel threatened yourself in terms of one or more of them. If so, it's likely that this emotion is having a strong impact on your interactions at work.

Communication Gaps

We as data scientists are great at analytic tasks, but we may need to work a bit harder to develop better listening skills. Many of us approach the negotiation so preoccupied with what we want to say that we fail to listen to what the other side is saying.

In his book, *Never Split the Difference*,[9] former FBI negotiator Chris Voss recommends that, instead of doing any thinking about our own arguments in the early negotiation stages, we focus solely on listening and understanding the other side. The insights we gain from these early efforts will help us frame our own future arguments, while our attentiveness will help us earn trust.

Remember that differences in language and culture can cause two people to hear the same words while understanding different meanings. So ask follow-up questions to validate you've understood each other correctly. Invite additional people you trust to your discussions and review notes together afterwards.

And be aware that people who appear to be cooperative may actually just be stalling, or they may even have no intention at all of reaching an agreement with you. I'll illustrate with an example.

> *In the situation I referred to above, where the first executive didn't want to share the data he managed, he directed his team to not share this data, while not*

---

[9] Voss, C., & Raz, T. (2016). *Never split the difference: Negotiating as if your life depended on it* [Kindle ed.]. Random House.

*actually saying that they wouldn't share it. In this
situation, the data stewards continued scheduling
meetings but would end each meeting with a request
for additional use case documentation. Initially, the
second team of data scientists responded by creating
and delivering the requested documents, but they
eventually realized that these additional requests were
simply stalling techniques. The data stewards couldn't
cooperate but didn't want to appear uncooperative.
This impasse continued until it was finally resolved
at the management level.*

This section explained several personal dimensions that can be barriers to your negotiation, and each may need to be resolved in a different way. But one of the most fundamental principles for establishing good communication with your colleagues is to make the effort to build strong, positive relationships with them from the start, before you come to the point of needing to work through difficult negotiations. Starting with a strong basis of trust and understanding will help you work through personal elements in conflicts and advance more quickly to the point of focusing on the problem.

Then Focus on the Problem

Now that I've discussed the need to address the human element, let's move on to the negotiation process itself. We typically enter a negotiation with certain goals in mind. I'll refer to these as the *positions* we take with respect to the negotiation.

In the example of salary negotiations, we might take a position such as "I would like a 10% salary increase." But upon reflection, what we really care about is that our hard work is recognized or that our career is progressing at pace, which are the real *interests* behind the position we've taken. You'll need to make a conscious decision— whether to remain fixed on your initial position or to reframe your negotiation in terms of your respective underlying interests.

Focus on the Underlying Interests

Of course by the time you realize that there's a disagreement, you and the other party have each already taken opposing positions. Perhaps you requested access to data or permissions on a system, additional responsibility, flexibility to work from home, or a promotion. But the other person didn't comply. You may have already started to argue in favor of your respective positions.

But take a step back from the positions on which you disagree and focus instead on your respective interests. By doing so, you may come to agreement much sooner. Let's continue with the salary example.

I've already listed a few interests that may be behind the data scientist's request for a salary increase (their position). The manager has taken the position that they don't want to give the 10% raise, but what might be their underlying interests? They might include:

1. A desire to keep salaries at consistent levels across the members of their team

2. A need to stay within the organization's guidelines for salary increases

3. Concern that the data scientist will not improve to their full potential if they're rewarded too highly for their current performance

4. Addressing current pressure on their team's budget

If you want to make real progress in the negotiation, start by identifying your own interests. Let go of your initial negotiating position and pursue your interests instead. And if both sides focus on interests instead of positions, you'll have a much better chance of reaching an agreement.

If you're negotiating in good faith—from a position of trust and mutual respect—you should each explain your underlying interests to the other. Making the switch from discussing positions to discussing interests can open up a world of alternative solutions for satisfying the interests of both sides. Now it's time to get creative.

Brainstorm Options That Work for Both Sides

Once you've identified each side's underlying interests, the next step is to think of creative solutions that could satisfy them—for both sides. Rather than negotiating toward a compromise in which each side gives up something, you want to work toward a win/win situation.

This process involves two steps: brainstorming possible solutions, and then, deciding which ones work best. We separate the brainstorming stage from the deciding stage by first having a session, possibly with a facilitator, where you together think creatively about possible solutions. At this point, you won't discuss or criticize ideas. Not every idea will be a good idea, and that's OK for now. Write all ideas out in full view as they're generated.

Brainstorming is followed by a decision stage, in which ideas may finally be criticized as they're refined into solutions that address the underlying interests of both sides. If this discussion is conducted in an honest and respectful manner, it can be a great opportunity for each side to further understand the other's underlying interests, which will in turn produce long-term benefits to your relationship.

Returning to our example, creative solutions to the salary negotiation could include:

1. The manager agrees to award a one-off bonus to the employee in recognition of exemplary performance on a specific project. (This was an option we had as management at eBay.) In this way, the employee feels recognized and valued, while the manager holds to the organization's salary bands.

2. The manager agrees to present benchmark salary studies provided by the employee to the human resources department and to request that HR increase salary bands for data scientist roles. In this way, the employee feels respected and validated by the manager, regardless of the final outcome.

3. The manager gives the employee additional responsibilities in a new area, thus helping the employee's career development.

An aside on this topic: I emphasize to junior data scientists in my trainings that they should ask for increases in responsibility, project experience and people management, rather than salary increases. A 10% salary increase within your current role pales in comparison to the salary leaps made as a data scientist progresses to senior, director, and VP levels, progressions which come only with experience and demonstrated performance. I'll return to this principle in chapter twelve.

In Conclusion

To negotiate effectively, start by identifying and addressing the personal elements—the motivations, perspectives and emotions—at play within the conflict. Next, as you address the topic of negotiation, you'll have a much better chance of arriving at a mutually beneficial solution when you apply the principles for open, unencumbered negotiation that I've described in this chapter. This more methodical, thoughtful approach requires considerable time and effort, but it pays off in a final outcome that's more likely to satisfy the interests of both sides, while increasing mutual understanding and trust.

Unfortunately, you'll sometimes find yourself in situations where the other party is unwilling to have such open discussions or to walk through the processes I've described. In practice, colleagues may dodge issues, ignore emails or not address topics in a straightforward manner. These are the most difficult conflicts to resolve—the ones that won't show their faces publicly. They constitute a portion of the opaque and intractable interactions we often refer to as "office politics." This is the subject of the next chapter.

Additional Reading

Fisher, R., Ury, W. L., & Patton, B. (2011). *Getting to yes: Negotiating agreement without giving in* (3rd rev. ed.). Penguin Books.

Voss, C., & Raz, T. (2016). *Never split the difference: Negotiating as if your life depended on it* [Kindle ed.]. Random House.

Bolton, R. (1986). *People skills: How to assert yourself, listen to others, and resolve conflicts.* Simon & Schuster.

· · · ·

CHAPTER FIVE

Navigating Office Politics

"Office politics" is a catch-all term that people tend to use when they don't like or understand a corporate decision. The term is especially useful when they feel they've been unfairly treated, perhaps as the victim of someone's animosity. In this chapter, I'll try to clarify which situations are most often labeled as "office politics" and then provide some advice for data scientists in navigating such situations.

Although everyone gets blindsided by office politics at some point in their career, data scientists are in some ways especially ill-prepared to navigate the unspoken rules and conflicting agendas so common within the corporate world (more on this in a bit). Although a handful of your colleagues may leverage office politics to advance their careers and increase their power, I'll assume you'd prefer to focus on the data science and simply need some perspective, along with a few basic survival skills.

My opinion is that much (but not all) of what we call "office politics" is the natural result of miscommunication and misunderstandings. I'll start by breaking the concept of office politics into two components: misperceptions (unintentional) and conflicting or hidden agendas (intentional).

Misperceptions

How You Are Evaluated

One reason I loved math in school was that it was clear when I was right and when I was wrong. (This changes when you get to graduate-level math.) What I didn't like about corporate life was that I'd sometimes receive criticism that I felt was unsubstantiated.

But that's how corporate life works. Although most people and organizations will try to be fair and objective, they'll typically have only a limited understanding of the quality of your work. The reality is that people will generally evaluate you based on three criteria:

1. Their understanding of the actual quality of your work

2. The (mis-)perceptions they form based on what they observe, such as perceiving you to be an expert coder because you write many lines of code

3. Input they receive from people they trust: your colleagues, your stakeholders and, above all, your manager

It's not difficult to see where this process can go wrong. Relatively few of the people you work with understand the quality of your work as a data scientist. They'll instead rely on their (mis-)perceptions, which are strongly influenced by their backgrounds and past experiences.

They'll also rely on input from your colleagues—input that may itself be based on (mis-)perceptions. Even worse, when providing input, a colleague may invent something that suits their own interests. That brings us to the second component of office politics: the hidden agenda, which I'll talk about in the second half of this chapter.

Why Data Scientists Are Especially Vulnerable

As data scientists, we're used to working with clear standards of success. We succeeded in school by solving clearly defined problems, evaluated in a fair and precise manner by domain experts (our instructors). It didn't matter how we dressed, if we drifted off during class or if we were ever-so-slightly rude to our teachers (on occasion).

In our math classes, we hardly needed to worry about perceptions or hidden agendas, and when we entered the workforce, we kept this heads-down focus, working in amazing concentration for hours or days on end. When we did leave our desks to interact with our nontechnical colleagues, we found the "apple/orange" effect. Our colleagues didn't understand the funny slogans on our T-shirts, and we'd never heard of the social influencers they were talking about.

But now we're noticing that there's a cost to not paying enough attention to people around us. We miss the subtle cues that someone may not be acting in a trustworthy manner (hidden agendas) or that we may have just left a bad impression on a colleague.

How Your Colleagues Perceive You

I talked about cultural differences before covering office politics because there's substantial overlap between these two topics. The challenge with cultural differences is that we often assume everyone does or should have the same values, making it easy to misjudge the character of a colleague from a different culture. But cultures aren't delineated solely by national borders. Geographic regions, ethnicities, social strata and even individual families each have their own subcultures. Companies also develop corporate cultures, some of which can be quite strong.

For example, we might assume that the colleague who leaves early for a family event doesn't care about their work. Or we assume the one who talks about their past accomplishments is egotistical; the one who starts meetings with ten minutes of idle chatter is unfocused; or, on the flip side, the one who gets straight to business without small talk is rude.

Such misperceptions are by no means limited to cultural differences. I wrote in chapter two about how different functional areas within an organization can each have their own sets of values. They often also have their own ways of perceiving actions, as I'll illustrate with an example.

> *A software developer I worked with decided one day to bring his own super-sized monitors to work. He did this so that he could be more productive, as he wanted to view his code, documentation and debugging windows all at once. Although this reasoning was clear to other software developers, his business colleagues across the room, who had no understanding of his screen space needs, felt he was simply showing off his monitors. They formed a negative perception of his character based on a misunderstanding of the reason for his actions. They passed on their misperception in the form of a character judgment when they later gave performance feedback on that employee.*

Such misperceptions are often labeled as "office politics." First, we make an unconscious judgment, not realizing we may have misperceived something about our colleague. After the misperception, we repeat our judgment to colleagues. One or more of these colleagues decide that this opinion could help them to advance their hidden agenda, so they further encourage its spread. A consensus opinion of the "victim" begins to form within the office, and decisions are made accordingly (being passed over for promotion, receiving negative performance reviews, etc.).

> *A company I once worked for had put customer satisfaction at the heart of its corporate strategy. To ingrain a certain servile attitude, the company didn't give its employees concrete objectives, but evaluated them twice per year purely on the basis of anonymous, subjective feedback from their colleagues. This in itself is actually not so uncommon, although most companies won't acknowledge how subjective their evaluation methods actually are. What was unusual in this company was that management openly told employees, "In this company, perception is what matters." I learned to make it a point to overcommunicate when I thought there might be a risk of misperception. For example, if I needed to leave early, I made very sure that everyone on my immediate team knew I would be working from home in the evening. In this regard, it was a miserable place for me, as a data scientist, to work, but it did teach me to be continually conscious of how others around me might be perceiving my actions.*

As a data scientist, you're already at a disadvantage because you're inclined to focus more on the work than on the perceptions of the people around you. In the corporate world, you have the additional disadvantage that no one understands what you do. Your colleagues have little or no basis for evaluating your work, so they rely on less-meaningful observations. If you come to work a bit late, sit at your desk working alone, pick up your phone regularly to reply to text messages, and then leave the office a bit early, the only observation your colleagues can make is that you don't seem to work as hard as they do.

I once fielded a complaint about a PhD data scientist I was managing. People had observed him taking more breaks than they did. The data scientist explained to me that the intense mental work required the frequent recharge. This made sense to me, but not to his colleagues.

In another company, the manager of a (nonanalytic) department came to me concerned that one of my junior data scientists, who happened to sit close to him, was checking social media too often.

Whether you spend fifteen minutes fitting a linear regression followed by two hours putting together a nice presentation or fifteen days fitting a neural network followed by fifteen minutes putting together a sloppy presentation, the only thing your business colleagues will see is how good the presentation looks.

Be aware that everything you do is making an impression on people around you: appearing distracted, irritable moods, time spent on social media and even poor hygiene can all sabotage your career by giving your colleagues a poor impression of you. Remember, when your colleagues don't understand your technical skills, they'll revert to meaningless ways to evaluate you.

Unfortunately, you can also lose points if you come across as too smart, too hardworking, or too energetic. People may see such actions as countercultural, or they may begin to perceive you as a threat, bringing you afoul of one of the most common hidden agendas—personal advancement.

> *I once helped an Asian analyst get a job at a*
> *European company. A month later, his new manager*
> *told me in confidence that his teammates were*
> *complaining to her that he was working too hard.*
> *The new colleague didn't last long in the position.*

I'll give some tips later in this chapter for managing your colleagues' perceptions.

Agendas

With the term "agenda," I mean the goals and objectives that influence our actions. Misperceptions, as I just discussed, are usually innocent, or at least unintentional, assumptions. Agendas are quite different. We each consciously create our own agendas, and we choose if and how to disclose them to others.

People will be transparent regarding some agendas, such as wanting to increase company revenue, reduce waste or finish a meeting on time. But they keep other agendas hidden, such as seeking their own promotion or taking revenge on a colleague. Let's look at two of the most common agenda-related problems you're likely to encounter as a data scientist.

Conflicting Agendas

People often use the term "office politics" when they observe conflicting agendas at play—when leadership tries to meet multiple objectives or to keep several parties happy at the same time. Being the analytically minded people we are, data scientists like to have clear, focused decision-making criteria, so we often complain when the basis for making a decision or evaluation is not what we feel it should be. If it's not transparent or if we feel it makes no sense, we are especially likely to call it "office politics."

If I work for a subsidiary of Yum! Brands and we're going to order pizza for a team event, no one is going to be surprised that we order from Pizza Hut (a Yum! Brands subsidiary), even if a better pizza shop is right next door. Here, we've balanced multiple agendas in a transparent way (company loyalty outweighs better pizza). Even if I'm not happy about the pizza, I understand the process.

But say my manager promotes my colleague instead of me even though I'm the one who best met the promotion criteria. It may be that this colleague just received a job offer from a competitor, and my manager is trying hard to keep him on board (without telling the rest of the team). In this case, my manager has conflicting agendas that aren't transparent to the team.

Although every decision needs to be balanced against multiple criteria, you as a data scientist operating in your own technical bubble can't possibly be aware of all the factors that influence decisions across your organization. You may complain that office politics was the reason why you didn't receive that promotion, or why your favorite project was terminated or why your desk was moved to the basement the same week that your software purchase wasn't approved, but each of those decisions was made by people who undoubtedly needed to balance multiple agendas, transparent to them but unknown to you. These people made the best decision they could to balance those agendas.

Or it could be that you simply don't agree with the basis for a decision. You want to code a project in Julia rather than Python (since Julia is obviously a better programming language in so many ways). Your manager says you need to keep developing in Python because blah, blah, blah … (You've tuned them out by this point.) You can call this office politics, but it's not. It's simply something you don't agree with.

Hidden Agendas

Certain agendas and decision criteria will always remain unspoken in the office. No one is going to admit when they're acting out of selfishness, spite or insecurity. Hidden agendas such as these are the most unpleasant component of office politics. People are unique, but hidden agendas are generally not, so it's possible to develop a sense of what to look out for. This will decrease the chance you'll get blindsided.

Remember the core human interests I listed when I talked about reaching agreement in the last chapter? Those five (autonomy, appreciation, affiliation, role and status) will almost never be vocalized, but you'll see them play out in the hidden agendas of your colleagues.

> *A company I worked for had acquired a smaller company and asked me to work with a manager in the acquired company to merge his department into mine. Not surprisingly, the second manager, faced with the prospect of soon losing his role, made it his unspoken mission to block the project in any way possible.*

As another example, consider a manager asked to provide input on a colleague put up for promotion. This manager may give negative feedback about the colleague simply because the manager doubts the degree to which this colleague would support the manager's work if that colleague were given the increased influence and responsibility.

For many people, the most important item on their (hidden) agenda is preserving or increasing their own power (possibly by hiding their incompetence). People like this won't support you or your work if they perceive you as a threat.

Fortunately, once you're aware of the danger of such misperceptions and hidden agendas, you can start to take evasive actions.

Self-Defense for Office Politics

Office politics is a complex issue with many influences and manifestations. There's no foolproof way to protect yourself from falling victim, but following some basic principles will help.

Stay Alert

Act and communicate in a way that minimizes the potential of creating a misperception. Stay alert for hidden agendas operating around you. Don't assume that all of your colleagues support you or that you all have the same goals.

Be especially vigilant when you sense resistance or hostility, as what you see may be only the tip of the iceberg. Try to understand the unseen part of this iceberg and take action before it sinks your project and possibly also your future prospects within the organization.

Typically, the first sign of hostility you'll notice will be downstream from the source. If someone is hostile toward you or perhaps even trying to sabotage your efforts, they'll often act behind your back rather than in full view. It's the people they've already worked to influence who'll first appear visibly hostile. If you've formed strong relationships with your colleagues, one of them will (hopefully) alert you when negative currents begin to flow through the office, giving you more advance warning.

I'll illustrate with an example:

> *A few years ago, I was working on a project at a company when my work suddenly brought to light a costly mistake one of the company directors had made.*

A few weeks later, the CTO of the company mentioned to me in our weekly meeting that he'd recently heard a number of complaints about my work. The complaints were unsubstantiated, but they each could have caused damage if taken at face value, and they needed to be addressed. (An example was the claim that key people hadn't been invited to certain meetings, which wasn't true.)

I was surprised that no one had brought these concerns directly to me, but I soon realized that all of those complaints had originated from the direct reports of the director who'd recently lost face because of my discovery. It seemed to be a subversive attempt to discredit me.

Fortunately, the CTO trusted me and brought the issues to me directly rather than simply accepting and possibly acting on them. I made an appointment to talk with the primary instigator, thinking we could discuss her complaints in our meeting. To my surprise, she brushed off the concerns she'd expressed to others in private and had nothing critical to say to me directly, neither in that meeting nor later.

It was the strong relationships I had already formed within the company (with the CTO in this case) that enabled me to successfully navigate that situation.

As this example illustrates, it always helps to have earned the trust of more senior colleagues, as they're in the best positions both to know what's being said within the organization and to mitigate the impact of any misinformation that's being spread.

Earn Credit

One way to protect yourself is to "bank" goodwill. Start any new role by making a conscious effort to earn respect and trust from your colleagues. They will then more readily give you the benefit of the doubt in their perceptions and are more likely to "have your back" if they see you running afoul of someone's hidden agenda.

To earn their trust and respect, start by:

1. **Investing time in building relationships**
   View break periods as opportunities to build relationships. Strike up conversations at the water cooler or coffee machine. Take the initiative and get to know people from other departments. Invest time in light conversation, taking interest in their personal lives as appropriate.

2. **Inspiring loyalty**
   Help others when you see the opportunity. Make their problems yours (to a certain degree). Work to protect the image of your colleagues. Be positive about them in public and defend their character and their work when possible. Respect work that has been done by others.

3. **Demonstrating your work ethic**
   Deliver on your commitments. Be honest about your mistakes. Volunteer for small, unglamorous tasks that others don't want to do.

4. **Communicating wisely**
   Emails should be factual and generally not contain anything that could embarrass you or others if made public. Don't use emails to vent emotions—it's too easy to create misunderstandings and to escalate conflict. When volunteering ideas,

be careful that you don't come across as a know-it-all.
(More on this in the next section.)

Consider such efforts at building trust to be a part of your basic job description.

Manage Perceptions

Another part of your self-imposed job description should be to actively manage the perceptions of those around you.

As I touched on earlier, take care that your colleagues don't perceive you as a threat. Stay humble. Always publicly acknowledge the accomplishments of your colleagues and pass credit to them whenever possible.

> *A colleague recounted to me the time when his previous department chose him for a four-week "high potential" program. The manager (foolishly) announced to the rest of his team that this person had been selected above them because he was so "exceptional." One teammate in particular would barely speak to him again after that announcement. This, despite the fact that my friend had not in the least promoted himself or bragged about the selection.*

Be very selective about when and where you practice self-promotion. I pointed out in chapter three that certain cultures view self-promotion as inherently wrong, while others admire people who sell themselves strongly. The latter will even assume that, if you have nothing great to say about yourself, then there must indeed be nothing great about you.

As a general principle, publicly promote the accomplishments of your team rather than your own accomplishments, and learn the culturally appropriate ways to self-promote when presenting yourself to new contacts or potential employers.

As your colleagues get to know you, they should also form the following basic impressions of you:

1. **Someone they want to sit next to.** It sounds obvious, but people want to work with people who are pleasant to have around. You'd be surprised how many hiring decisions are based on this simple factor. Even after you've got the job, people who find you obnoxious or unfriendly are less likely to give you the benefit of the doubt or have your back.

2. **Someone who "gets" how things work.** Learn the company culture—the basics of how things work there. Is your company high power distance or high uncertainty avoiding? Are decisions made by consensus during meetings or in private conversations after the meeting? Does management welcome open debate or expect public agreement? Is it a fun-loving culture? Are there certain social events that are important to attend? Learning such nuances will demonstrate your ability to thrive in your new environment.

3. **Someone who adds business value.** Tune in to what nontechnical colleagues see as important, and don't keep pushing ideas if no one else sees them as having business value. Catch the ball when there's an emergency. Focus on tasks that are important to your company now, even if it means diverting effort from tasks you'd prefer to work on.

Gatekeepers and Trusted Advisors

As I mentioned earlier, senior managers often rely on trusted advisors to help them form opinions and make decisions. These advisors may be the people reporting to them directly, or they may be others in the company who have, over time, earned their trust. For example, the programmer who has worked quietly in the corner for the past ten years may be the person your director goes to when they're making a decision related to technology. Trusted advisors are often also the gatekeepers who can open doors for requests or new ideas.

Gatekeepers and trusted advisors in your organization can be your strongest advocates when situations arise in which you or your work are threatened in some way. They can also give valuable early feedback on your ideas and initiatives.

Your most important gatekeeper and trusted advisor is your own line manager. This is one of many reasons to make sure you're having regular meetings with them. During these meetings, your manager should pass on to you anything significant they've heard about how people are perceiving you—whether it's positive or negative. Your annual review shouldn't be the only time you receive such feedback.

In Conclusion

Since I first began talking about office politics in my trainings several years ago, I've heard mixed reactions. Some data scientists are enthusiastic to finally see the topic addressed. Others don't perceive it as such an important subject. I expect the reactions differed based on the organizational cultures in which they've worked, as well as their level of seniority.

In my personal experience, the organizational interactions commonly filed under the umbrella term "office politics" do indeed play a crucial role in the success of analytic initiatives. You will never completely understand all the agendas and perceptions at play around you, but training yourself to be observant and to follow certain best practices can help minimize the chance of getting sunk by that iceberg. Realize that your technical skills and talents are no longer all that matter. If you don't have the support of the people around you, you will fail.

Additional Reading

Shapiro, C. (2005). *Corporate confidential: 50 secrets your company doesn't want you to know—and what to do about them.* St. Martin's Griffin.

Brandon, R., & Seldman, M. (2004). *Survival of the savvy: High-integrity political tactics for career and company success.* Free Press.

Storytelling

CHAPTER SIX

Constructing Your Message

Possibly the most important business skill for data scientists is the ability to communicate their achievements and insights, especially to nontechnical audiences. You've probably already learned to use plotting libraries such as Shiny or Seaborn, but these technical skills are just the start. You'll also need to understand how to refine and communicate the story of your work, to allow you to demonstrate its value and motivate your audience to action.

To properly cover the topic of communication, I want to discuss three skills:

1. Understanding your audience (Who)
2. Developing your story (What)
3. Delivering your insights (How)

This chapter will cover the **Who** and **What** questions, as well as a portion of the **How**. The next chapter will go into more technical detail regarding the **How**.

Understanding Your Audience (Who)

Remember that a key theme in this book is that we should always try to understand the perspectives of our colleagues. This is especially critical when we're communicating about our work in the form of a presentation.

As you begin preparing a presentation, ask yourself the following questions:

1. **Who is my target audience?**

   As I discussed in chapter two, your colleagues will have various priorities, technical backgrounds and business specializations. Most likely, there will be a variety of people in the room or copied on the email, so you'll need to choose who in particular you'll target and adjust your presentation to best suit their priorities and backgrounds. Generally, you'll choose either the primary stakeholder or the most senior decision maker in the room as your target audience. However, remember that in the case of low power distance cultures, the more junior staff may be the real decision makers.

2. **What is the current mindset of my target audience?**

   Most data scientists I work with don't consider this question, so I try to hammer it in. Remember in chapter two we saw that increased seniority means more responsibility for increasingly diverse projects. So, imagine you're a senior manager opening your inbox at 8:20 a.m. You've got twenty-five new emails and ten minutes before your first of a dozen meetings. That's twenty-four seconds per email, one of which is a project update from a data scientist. Twenty-four seconds to switch gears and remember what the project was even about, understand the update, filter out any action required and take that action. Now, imagine you're a data scientist composing an email to that manager. Remember those twenty-four seconds before you click "Send."

The CEO of a very large company once confided to me that he would typically read only the first and last three words of each paragraph. It was one of the ways he'd learned to navigate the overwhelming number of documents he needed to review.

This is why written updates and presentations sent to senior management need to be powerfully concise and crystal clear in terms of both message and requests.

If you're presenting in person, you're in a slightly better situation in that the attendee has, in principle, allocated a larger amount of time to your presentation. However, you still need to keep in mind that the target audience may be near brain-dead following a stream of exhausting meetings and will likely arrive at your meeting having neither read the background documentation nor even remotely thought about the topic you'll be discussing. You'll need to help motivate that person or group of people to switch gears and care about what you're going to discuss. (I'll get into this more in the "how" chapter.)

Or your target audience may care very much about your work. They may have high expectations for your results. Or they may have a preconceived negative opinion of your work, in which case your goal becomes less to capture their attention than to quickly and effectively address the concerns that are top of mind for them at the moment.

3. **What is important to my target audience?**
As I mentioned in chapter two, different types of colleagues will appreciate different elements in a presentation.

If you're addressing another data scientist, they'll be interested in your methodology, the technology you used and the resulting metrics you achieved.

However, if your audience is from another business unit, they'll be interested in how you've impacted their KPIs. For example, how did you increase conversion rates or reduce costs? What new business insights have you discovered? They probably won't understand or care about which tools or methods you've used, so put all this information in the appendix.

If your audience is an executive, they'll probably also be looking to understand the big picture of how data science is producing value in the organization and where it can be applied within other departments. They may also be interested in organizational questions, such as how effectively departments are collaborating or whether you're hitting organizational roadblocks.

Here's a quick summary of what different audiences are looking for:

- Data scientists want to see model metrics.
- Finance wants to see tables, exact numbers and very specific details (exact date of the figures, data source, etc.).
- Marketing expects a visually polished presentation.
- Strategists expect insights and recommendations presented as compelling charts.
- Executives expect clear summaries and takeaways (including an executive summary, which I'll discuss later).

4. **What is the technical background of my audience?**
   You've spent years in your area of specialization, but your target audience is probably not even familiar with the basic

terminology. Even if your audience has a technical background, as is the case when you present to software developers
or even to data scientists working on other topics, they can
still very easily get lost in specialized terminology.

Your audience will probably have no idea what the difference
is between precision and recall. If your message to them is
that the model is much better, just pick one metric and report
on it. And don't spend five minutes trying to introduce the
F1 score to them, unless they absolutely need to understand
the F1 score (for some unimaginable reason). Carefully
consider what terminology your audience will already be
comfortable with and try to limit yourself to that terminology,
even if it pains you to oversimplify. Put the rest in the
appendix.

Tips for Understanding a New Audience

If you're presenting to an unfamiliar group or department, you'll need
to adapt your presentation style for an audience of strangers. This is
often the case, for example, if your project is getting broader exposure
within the organization and you're asked to introduce it to more senior executives or to a wider audience.

When I prepare for a target audience I haven't worked with in the
past, I generally follow two additional principles:

1. **Try to connect ahead of time with one or more people
   who have experience with this audience.** I'll ask what style
   and content work best for that person or group. After I've
   prepared a draft of the presentation, I'll ask my advisor for
   feedback. In many cases, your immediate manager will be
   the person best positioned to give you that advice.

> *I recently ran a project helping a company form their strategy for machine learning and AI, with my primary point of contact being the Chief Product Officer (CPO). A few months into the project, I was scheduled to summarize results to the C-suite. After preparing the presentation, I sat down with the CPO for an hour to review. She very helpfully pointed out that certain elements of the framework I was using would not, in her opinion, be intuitive to her colleagues. I incorporated her input, and the presentation to her colleagues ended up going smoothly.*

2. **Keep the primary content in your initial presentation at a high level, but place most supporting and/or technical data in the appendices.** This will allow you to communicate your main message without getting bogged down in details that your audience may not understand or be interested in. At the same time, the appendices demonstrate that you've done the work and allow you to flip forward as specific questions arise. Once you've learned which details seem important to your audience, you can begin to incorporate them in the main content in subsequent presentations.

Forming Your Story (What)

We can't communicate clearly until we clearly understand what we want to communicate. Richard Feynman has been quoted as saying that if he couldn't explain a principle of physics at the freshman level, it meant he must not really understand it.[10] We often find ourselves in this situation with our data science projects. We begin working on a project based on a somewhat vague initial idea, but we don't take

---

[10] Goodstein, D. L., and Goodstein, J. R. (1996). *Feynman's lost lecture: The motion of planets around the sun.* California Institute of Technology.

the time to really get clear in our own minds what exactly we're doing and why we're doing it. The more I see of data science projects within organizations, the more I realize how shockingly often we data scientists work on projects with no clearly defined story.

The Three-Minute Story

If you've had a chance to read the book *Storytelling with Data*,[11] you'll see how the author recommends that, when you give a presentation, you also write a summary that you can recount in three minutes. This summary should include:

1. An introduction/background context
2. The topic of importance (e.g., the business challenge, framed in terms familiar to your audience)
3. The goal: What needs to change?
4. The solution: How will (or did) you bring about the changes?

Within data science projects, it's possible that your first occasion to prepare a three-minute summary will be when you're introducing your project at something like a department-level meeting, or whichever type of presentation is one level up from a Sprint demo in your company. You probably won't have completed the project by then, but you should be in a position to describe your motivation as well as your vision to an audience not yet familiar with the project. You should simultaneously prepare both a full presentation and a three-minute summary of that presentation.

I've personally found the process of formulating such a three-minute story to be enormously helpful for clarifying in my own mind what I'm doing and why. But constructing such a summary is a lot

---

[11] Knaflic, C. N. (2015). *Storytelling with data: A data visualization guide for business professionals.* John Wiley & Sons, Inc.

harder than it sounds. In the past, I've spent over an hour creating a single, concise, three-minute story for a presentation, even after I'm already deep into the project.

But the process is worth it. Your three-minute story will be useful in several ways:

- It will force you to clarify in your own mind the four elements listed above.

- It can serve as the executive summary for your project's final presentation and as a high-level project summary when your team or department is presenting an overview of recent work.

- It prepares you for water-cooler moments, when you run into a colleague who asks what you're working on.

- It prepares you for those all-too-common moments when you're scheduled for the last twenty-minute slot but are only given the floor with five minutes remaining.

Oddly enough, I recently found myself in this exact situation. I was asked to present my team's work during the last twenty-five minutes of a department-wide meeting. Coincidentally, I had just given a training in which I'd explained the concept of the three-minute story, so I found it somewhat ironic when my colleague overran his allotted time and left me with about four minutes for my presentation. Although I had my three-minute version ready, I did manage to negotiate for ten minutes, allowing me to elaborate a bit on the three-minute version by highlighting some key slides from the longer presentation. I actually got very positive feedback after the presentation, but I was only able to shorten it on the spot in this way because the core story was already clear and well-prepared in my own mind.

To give you a concrete example, here is that (redacted) three-minute story:

BACKGROUND

Because digital marketing drives XXX percent of our gross revenue, our marketing department is continually developing ways to excel in it. Even as we invest substantial resources to fund and operate campaigns for acquisition or retargeting, we find that an advertising landscape fragmented across Google, Facebook, Pinterest and a dozen other platforms, and complicated by recent developments such as GDPR and ITP2.2, has increased the workload and complexity required. This pushes us to explore more sophisticated techniques for digital marketing.

IMPORTANCE

We need to target the right audience at the right time and would even like to employ sophisticated machine learning algorithms to increase marketing ROI. If campaigns always require extensive manual effort, we will not be able to quickly adjust to changing market conditions. We also look to develop ways to answer specific questions about customer behavior and intent, enabling us to approach customers in more relevant ways.

GOAL

Project YYY promises to enable better acquisition and retargeting across our advertising networks, as well as automation and increased scalability for campaigns. It also provides tools and technologies for building advanced machine learning models for precision targeting. The goal of this project is to build the technical foundations and implement several proofs of concept to demonstrate its potential to improve targeting, activation and analysis in a scalable and maintainable manner.

STATUS

We have already laid much of the required technical foundation and are in the process of adding data sources chosen for specific applications. We have begun benefitting from several out-of-the-box targeting and activation features and have also built XXX (our own targeting and activation machine learning models). Over the coming months, we plan to finalize the technical foundations and deploy YYY for use in campaigns in markets ZZZ.

The Recommendation

The three-minute story is an important tool when you're presenting a project or recommending an initiative, both of which require a storytelling framework. But sometimes you're asked to complete a piece of analysis independent of the larger picture, or perhaps to simply assemble specific data into a report for someone else to analyze. If you find you're often given these types of tasks, you should work hard to rebrand yourself as a business thought partner, rather than simply a data monkey.

How do we brand ourselves as thought partners?

A common mistake junior analysts make is to spend hours or days collecting, analyzing and preparing presentations without preparing an insight or recommendation. It's a sign of immaturity, and it drives senior management crazy.

> *In a private conversation at a brand you've all heard of, one of the VPs lamented to me how his analysts only provide him with reports, not with opinions or insights.*

You may view your job in terms of SQL queries, correlation analysis and model fitting, but your business audience ultimately cares about none of these. They care about a business insight—what did we discover about customer shopping habits that we didn't know before? They care about recommendations for action—which marketing channel is draining budget but not producing results?

My advice to data scientists is to not just report on what you did and how you did it, but to also share insights and prepare recommendations. You may be the person in your company best placed to find new insights because you have the fullest access to the data and to the tools best able to explore that data.

As you carry out the requests of your stakeholders, take the initiative to ask deeper and wider questions about the data you're working with. Try different sets of dependent variables and different bins and groupings. Use different types of charts to visualize your data (more about this later). Exploring different sets of data and different chart types will reveal insights you may not have seen in your initial analysis.

Even if your audience doesn't want your opinion (for whatever reason), you should still take the time to form an opinion. Why?

1. The process itself will help you find mistakes in your analysis and will encourage you to more fully understand the data and business setting, steering you toward better analysis in the future.

2. In the event that you **are** asked for an opinion, you'll be prepared. If they ask and you aren't, you've lost what could have been a career-building opportunity.

3. You'll be prepared to more intelligently discuss your past work when interviewing for future jobs. Seriously.

But be cautious when considering if and how to communicate the opinion you've formed. Certain people and cultures may find it presumptuous for junior staff to volunteer recommendations before they're asked. Your recommendation might also touch on a topic with sensitivities you're not aware of. It's generally good practice to let your manager review your recommendations before you present them.

If you plan to recommend something that's likely to be controversial, it can help greatly if you find opportunities to "pre-present" your analysis and recommendations. First, show your presentation to a knowledgeable person you trust. This person can point out flaws in your arguments or highlight issues that are likely to cause dissension in your audience. Even better, try to walk through your presentation ahead of time with someone who will actually be part of your audience. If that participant already understands and supports your recommendation going into your presentation, they can help you explain your points and support your case when questions arise.

Communicating Your Story (How)

As a data scientist, you probably enjoy the modeling and the coding more than other tasks. It's easy to consider a presentation as a necessary evil that you'd like to be done with as quickly as possible.

However, you should view your presentations as one of your most important project deliverables. They're important for several reasons:

1. **Presentations sell your project.** You need to present your work well if you want it to get used. Presentations are your opportunity to tell your colleagues and managers what you've done and why it's important. Your work will be useless until others in your organization buy into it, add their unique input, and run with it.

2. **Presentations demonstrate your value.** You've just spent weeks doing work that few of your colleagues understand. Presentations are your chance to demonstrate your hard

work and initiative by explaining what you've been busy with and why it was challenging.

3. **Presentations enhance your own understanding.** You'll benefit from the process of preparing a presentation. It takes effort to prepare a good presentation. You need to clarify your thoughts, compose the text, create the graphics and consider questions you might be asked. This preparation process can be enormously beneficial, both in helping you think about the project in new ways and in providing you with material that you can reuse as you discuss the project in future presentations and conversations.

The more you improve your presentation skills, the more comfortable you'll be preparing and delivering future presentations. I've known analysts who enjoyed this part of their work so much that they now work exclusively on visuals and presentations. In the next chapter, I'll talk about how to design better slides and graphics. But before we get to that, let's look at three basic guidelines for communicating your work.

Make It Clear

As a data scientist, you probably have an above-average ability to grasp technical concepts and to analyze data quickly. So keep this in mind—what takes you five seconds to understand might take your nontechnical audience thirty seconds.

Add to this the fact that your audience is busy. They haven't thought about your project in the days or weeks leading up to the point where they've sat down in the meeting or opened your email, and they don't have the energy to stare at your analysis for thirty seconds to try to fish out your main points. Every piece of communication you send should have a takeaway message, request or proposal that will be obvious to your audience within just a few seconds.

In practical terms, this means that a slide title should generally be the main takeaway from the slide; for example, "Sales Are Down in Europe," not "Sales Results in Europe." Insights on a graph should jump out immediately (possibly through annotation). Show the chart to your analyst colleague. If your teammate doesn't see the insight within three seconds, your audience won't see it in five.

Multipage presentations **must** start with executive summaries. An executive summary is a single slide that summarizes your presentation, including the results, insights and recommendations. Increase the scanability of this slide by breaking details into paragraphs and using bold font for key phrases. In the next chapter, I'll introduce the concept of visual hierarchy, along with techniques for how to create visual hierarchies in your slides.

Make It Interesting

If you haven't already seen it, search for the TED Talk by Hans Rosling entitled "The Best Stats You've Ever Seen." I often use this talk as an illustration during my trainings.

You'll see in this talk how Rosling demonstrates tremendous enthusiasm for his topic. He's exceptionally lively and animated, and it's tempting to attribute the impact of his talk to this animation. But watch Sir Ken Robinson's TED talks, and you'll see equally effective communication by a man who stands fixed in place as he speaks with dry British humor. Though their delivery styles are different, what both speakers have in common is a strong passion for their subject matter, coupled with hard work in developing a captivating presentation.

How does this apply to us?

First, and foremost, you should yourself be interested in what you're presenting. If you're not excited about your message, you can't expect others to be. Take a few minutes to reflect on the analysis you've been asked to do:

- What parts of it are most interesting to you?
- What strikes you as unusual?
- What do you feel has the most potential to impact business results?
- What questions are left unanswered in your mind?

If you aren't able to get excited about your analysis and results, you have a deeper challenge than simply how to prepare this presentation.

Next, put yourself in the shoes of your audience and think what would most interest them. Remember the discussion in chapter two of how your colleagues in other business units differ. Think about how you can connect with their world and generate a shared excitement.

Be Prepared

Don't underestimate the importance of being prepared.

Preparation is especially critical for oral presentations, during which the most important aspect is having the story clear in your own mind. You can give a stunning oral presentation with minimalistic slides as long as you're clear and passionate about your message.

Never be caught mid-presentation trying to think what you want to say next. At any point in your presentation, you should know the content and the main message of your next slide before displaying it.

I talked about working to make the presentation interesting to your audience. If you watch the talks by Rosling or Robinson, you'll see how they're interspersed with illustrations and small jokes that work to maintain the attention of the audience and draw them in to the message of the presentation. Such components can be extremely valuable and will earn the respect of your audience, but they take time to generate.

When you're preparing written material, whether it be PowerPoint slides or an email summary, it will take time to construct a clear message. If it's an important piece of communication, you'll need to review it multiple times to catch mistakes, and then you'll want to pass it on to colleagues for review. If you present substandard quality material, your audience will consider you unprofessional. If you present material with spelling mistakes, your audience will consider you uneducated. If you present material with factual mistakes, your audience will consider you unreliable.

And find ways to keep their interest during what could otherwise be a dry or boring presentation. Intersperse a few content-light slides, use a bit of humor, and add human interest elements to help keep your audience engaged.

In Conclusion

You may dread giving presentations, but it's critical that you are able to clearly craft and deliver a story that helps your audience understand and get excited about the work you've been doing. This skill will win support for your project, and it will enhance your career.

In this chapter, I broke communication down into the elements of Who, What and How, continuing to expand on the key theme of empathizing with your colleagues' viewpoints—but also emphasizing the importance of developing your own understanding of and excitement for the message you're trying to share.

The next chapter will elaborate on techniques for graphs, tables and slides, showing how to more clearly communicate your insights in visual format.

CHAPTER SEVEN

Creating Effective Tables and Graphs

Nearly every data scientist I've worked with has at some point in their career consistently produced really awful charts. It's too bad that we spend months doing great work but then drop the ball when we try to show this great work to our colleagues.

But this chapter is not about how to make more elaborate or complicated graphs. It's quite the opposite. This chapter describes how to make your graphs as simple and straightforward as possible, with the goal of communicating your most important messages as quickly and intuitively as possible and with minimal visual distraction.

This chapter covers fundamental design principles you should use in every chart you produce as a data scientist. This is an expansive topic, and I'll only briefly touch on topics that have been covered extensively in large books devoted exclusively to the subject, such as the excellent books by Stephen Few. This is the longest chapter in the book. It may also be the one you'll start applying the soonest.

Our goal with charts is to make the right message jump out to a busy, possibly nontechnical audience as quickly and effortlessly as possible. In keeping with the core theme of this book, we'll always try to put ourselves in the shoes of our intended audience, trying to picture how they'll perceive our presentation, especially during the initial few seconds after they've first seen each page.

I'll present three skills:

1. **Choosing the right graph.** Consider whether a table or a graph best fits your message. Likewise, when using a graph, look to choose a design that's clear and easy to digest.

2. **Eliminating clutter.** Remove anything on your visual that's not absolutely necessary in making your point. This also applies to how big or thick you make chart elements, because bigger elements attract attention. Your goal is to reduce the ink-to-insight ratio of each visual.

3. **Making your message stand out.** Draw attention immediately to the most important elements. Construct visual layers (hierarchies) so that your audience can see the main points immediately and then choose how deep into the details to go.

As I elaborate on these skills, I'll introduce two helpful concepts of visual perception: **Gestalt principles** to help eliminate clutter, followed by **preattentive processing** to help make the primary message stand out.

I'll start by introducing preattentive processing, as I'll be referring to it throughout this chapter.

Preattentive Processing

The term preattentive processing refers to situations in which our minds collect and process information from our environment before we consciously focus our attention on it. Preattentive processing will be your new best friend when making data science presentations. I'll explain several ways you'll use it, but first let's see an example.

Try counting the 6's below, first in the left image and then in the right

94375565647473   94375565647473
58781875629114   58781875629114
42625931416389   42625931416389
69516537748762   69516537748762

Figure 11. Example of preattentive processing with digits

Notice how you can spot the 6's in the right image without any effort. This is preattentive processing.

We process several visual attributes preattentively, illustrated in Figure 12.

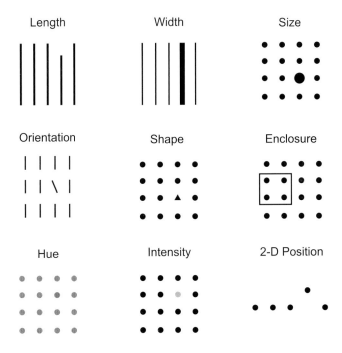

Figure 12. Preattentive visual attributes

Object motion is also preattentive (which is why we don't spot camouflaged animals until they move).

Preattentive Processing in Charts

You can utilize any one of these attributes to make a visual element stand out to your audience. We as data scientists are especially interested in ways to quickly communicate quantities so that our audience can immediately see which elements are bigger or smaller. This limits the attributes from which we can choose.

Only five of the preattentive attributes can be used to compare magnitudes. These are length, width, size, intensity and 2-D position. However, only length and 2-D position allow us to clearly distinguish small differences. Bar graphs work so well because we can instantly spot even small differences in length, but pie charts present the challenge that it's difficult to spot small differences in the width of pie segments.

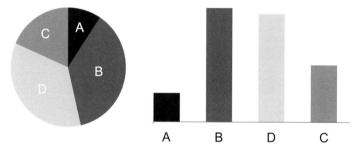

Figure 13. Comparing values is easier with bar graphs

Heat maps leverage the preattentive attribute of intensity. This makes them easier to scan (intensity jumps out), although small variations in cell intensity are difficult to distinguish.

34%	76%	57%	40%
13%	72%	86%	32%
61%	17%	26%	23%
50%	32%	47%	4%

Figure 14. Heat maps illustrate the attribute of intensity

Preattentive Processing in Text

As we saw with the initial example of 6's, adding preattentive attributes to text is a great way to make cells stand out in tables.

Consider the following text from one of Jeff Bezos's annual letters:[12]

> *Our first-party business has grown dramatically over that period, from $1.6 billion in 1999 to $117 billion this past year. The compound annual growth rate for our first-party business in that time period is 25%. But in that same time, third-party sales have grown from $0.1 billion to $160 billion—a compound annual growth rate of 52%.*

Did you feel the **cognitive load**—the effort it took you to extract meaning from this paragraph? Was there a main point? The reader might need to read this again to decide.

Now let's leverage different preattentive attributes to immediately draw the readers' attention to specific messages within the text.

First, I'll make part of the paragraph more intense (bold):

> Our first-party business has grown dramatically over that period, from $1.6 billion in 1999 to $117 billion this past year. The compound annual growth rate for our first-party business in that time period is 25%. But in that same time, third-party sales have grown from $0.1 billion to $160 billion— **a compound annual growth rate of 52%.**

---

[12] Bezos, J. (2018). Letter to shareholders.

Now I'll use enclosure:

> Our first-party business has grown dramatically over that period, from $1.6 billion in 1999 to $117 billion this past year. The compound annual growth rate for our first-party business in that time period is 25%. But in that same time, third-party sales have grown from $0.1 billion to $160 billion— a compound annual growth rate of 52%.

Now color (hue):

> Our first-party business has grown dramatically over that period, **from $1.6 billion in 1999 to $117 billion this past year.** The compound annual growth rate for our first-party business in that time period is 25%. But in that same time, third-party sales have grown from $0.1 billion to $160 billion— a compound annual growth rate of 52%.

Preattentive attributes work just as well for highlighting elements within tables and graphs, which I'll illustrate soon. But first you'll need to understand how to choose the type of chart best suited to your presentation.

Choosing the Right Chart

Tables vs. Graphs

First a word on terminology. Following convention used by Stephen Few (and others), I'll use the term "chart" to refer to a general visual representation of data—tables, diagrams or graphs, where the term "graph" is used for visualizations of data with lines, points, etc. This terminology may cause some confusion, as "pie charts" and "bar charts" are indeed charts but are, more specifically, graphs. Thus, not all charts are graphs, and, although the term "pie charts" is correct, we might more precisely call them "pie graphs."[13]

In my experience, data scientists typically default to using tables in their presentations and dashboards. This makes sense, as SQL queries spit out tables. In addition, the finance department generally wants data in tables. Since finance is typically the first stakeholder for your business intelligence systems, it may be that many or most of your reports are designed for their use. As you'll remember from chapter two, finance needs precise numbers, along with the ability to reference and compare different data points, so tables work well for them. Data scientists get used to delivering tables, and no one complains.

But don't default to using tables simply because it's easy or because your last stakeholder wanted a table. Make a conscious choice whether your message is best conveyed in a table or a graph. Think of it this way:

- Use tables when the message is contained in the exact numbers and when the numbers will be sequentially compared against each other.

- Use graphs when you want to illustrate patterns or visual relationships. Your mind will process insights much more quickly using graphs, so they're also great tools for data exploration.

Your audience will always need to exert mental effort to get information out of your presentation. I briefly introduced the concept of cognitive load earlier in this chapter. Your goal is to reduce cognitive

---

[13] I'll still refer to them as "pie charts" in this book.

load as much as possible, because the less cognitive load you inflict, the more likely you are to keep your audience's attention.

Tables tend to inflict higher cognitive load on your audience, as they generally present more information, in more detail, and with fewer visual guides. Basic graphs with minimal text, however, generally bring very little cognitive load, which makes them the best way to communicate simple messages. You'll need to decide if the additional information you can put into a table is worth the higher cognitive load.

To illustrate, consider the two financial charts in Figure 15.

YTD Sales

2020 Year-to-Date Sales

	As at Sept 15, 2020			Year-End Forecast		
	Units Sold	Percent of Total	Percent of Annual Plan	Budget	Forecast	vs Budget
Laptops	2,320	28%	68%	3,412	3,483	102%
Tablets	532	7%	62%	858	698	81%
Phones	5,299	65%	83%	6,384	8,254	129%
	8,151	100%	77%	10,654	12,436	117%

Figure 15. Comparison of financial data in a graph and a table

If your goal is simply to illustrate to your audience the large relative differences in device sales, the bar graph does this most efficiently. By leveraging the preattentive attribute of length, the bars instantly communicate this single message. If you instead used the table to present that simple message, the audience would need to find and mentally compare the relevant numbers, which would slow them down considerably and wear them out just a bit more. The extra details in the table would also distract from your message.

However, if your goal is to tell a longer or more specific story, the table may be the better choice. With a table, you can present precise numbers and communicate multiple messages—aggregates, percentages of total, relations to financial plans, etc. You could also simultaneously display multiple units of measurement, such as dollars, percentages and device units.

And so you see that either of these two charts could be appropriate for your report or presentation; the choice depends on your audience and on the message(s) you want to convey. For an open discussion of financial progress, you'd probably choose the table, but for a presentation where you wanted to quickly illustrate the relative magnitudes of each market and then move on to a further discussion, that same table would not be a good choice.

To illustrate with another example, have a quick glance at the table below and see what insights jump out.

What is your view of the UN?

	Unfavorable	Favorable
Argentina	26%	38%
Australia	32%	60%
Canada	26%	69%
Germany	27%	65%
India	14%	42%
Japan	35%	47%
Nigeria	25%	58%
Philippines	9%	86%
Russia	43%	34%
Turkey	54%	28%
US	33%	59%

Figure 16. Comparison using a data table[14]

It's quite possible that one of the first things you noticed was that the Philippines has the lowest number in the table (9%). But why did that low number stand out to you? Probably because of a visual cue—an indentation where the column changed from double to single digit. The preattentive attribute of length grabbed your attention.

---

[14] Source: Pew Research, 2019.

Here's the same information presented as a graph.

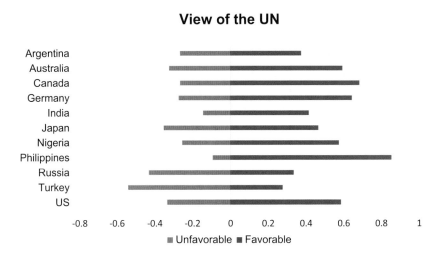

Figure 17. Comparison using bar graphs

Notice what a difference a graph makes in your ability to process the information. Because length is preattentive, we can quickly identify the largest and smallest values and can easily compare relative magnitudes.

In summary, use tables when

- Your audience will need to look up or compare values
- Precision is key to your message
- You need to show multiple units of measurement
- You want to show both individual and aggregate values

Use graphs when

- Your message is contained in the pattern (e.g., trends, orders of magnitude, **outliers**, exceptions)
- You're showing relationships within the bigger picture

Choosing between Graphs

When a graph **is** the right choice, how do you pick the right type of graph? You have a wide selection of possible graphs to choose from—scatterplots, line graphs, bar graphs, stacked bar graphs, pie charts, violin graphs, etc.—along with a choice for how to assign variables to axes.

Choose the chart that communicates your message most simply, typically leveraging preattentive attributes to do so. Here are some examples.

Scatter Plots

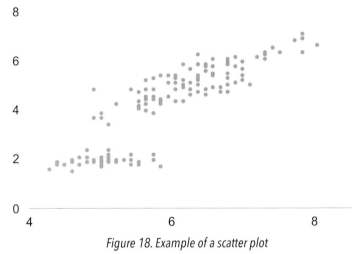

Figure 18. Example of a scatter plot

Scatter plots are the most basic and pure form of graph—they're the smallest step away from a raw table. They sacrifice a table's precision and ability to show multiple metrics and aggregates while providing in exchange the preattentive visual insights of two-dimensional position.

Scatter plots provide complete freedom to search for patterns and anomalies (such as the linearities illustrated above), as we haven't yet added connections, as with line graphs, nor the heavy visual emphasis that will come with bar graphs. Scatter plots provide a good resource for self-discovery but generally aren't as useful for communicating a message, such as an association between points.

Line Graphs

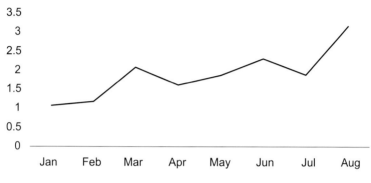

Figure 19. Example of a line graph

We often want to communicate that data points within scatter plots are associated in some way, such as when we're presenting time series data. One of the strongest ways to indicate association is to connect sets of data points with a line. (I'll return to this point when I introduce Gestalt principles in a few pages.) Line graphs make it extremely easy for our audience to see that association.

Bar Graphs (horizontal, vertical, waterfall, stacked)

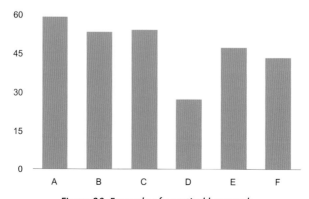

Figure 20. Example of a vertical bar graph

Bars do one thing extremely well: they make it easy to compare the magnitude of several data points. They do this by employing the preattentive attribute of length, emphasized with the visual weight of the bar. This approach works well if there are only a few data points, and if we care only about comparing one dimension.

But bar graphs don't work as well with multidimensional data. Analysts often use a stacked bar or waterfall in such cases, but once you start stacking bars, it becomes difficult to visually compare all but one or two of the groups (depending on whether you align at an endpoint or, rather, between categories).

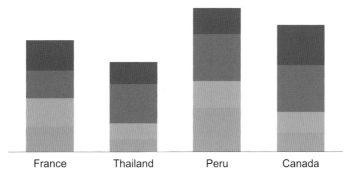

Figure 21. Upper layers are difficult to compare within stacked bars.

When using bar graphs, keep a few things in mind:

1. Always base the y axis of the graph at zero; otherwise, visual changes in magnitude are deceptive.

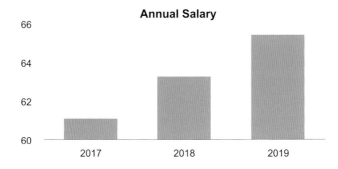

Figure 22. Bar graphs should show the zero-axis value, which is not shown here.

2. Don't rotate labels. Instead, either abbreviate or switch to a horizontal bar graph. A 1956 study showed that readers took over 50% longer to read text rotated 45° in either direction and over 200% longer to read text rotated at 90°.[15]

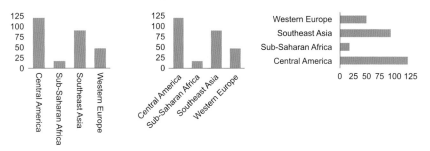

Figure 23. Use horizontal bars to avoid rotating text.

Slope Graphs

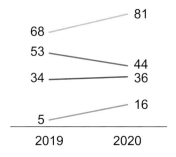

Figure 24. Example of a slope graph

Slope graphs can be used instead of bar graphs when we're comparing data points in sets of two. By removing the bars and connecting the data points with straight lines, we remove much of the clutter, keeping the ability to visually compare magnitudes but with less visual distraction.

[15] Tinker, M. (1956). Effect of angular alignment upon readability of print. *Journal of Educational Psychology*, 47(6), 358–363.

I'm a big fan of slope graphs. They're much more compact than bar graphs when comparing two categories or points in time.

Area Graphs (e.g., Pie Charts)

Visualization experts typically discourage the use of pie and similar area graphs (donut, tree map, etc.). I showed an example earlier in the chapter where a small difference in magnitude was easy to see with a bar graph but not with a pie chart.

People often remark that they appreciate how a pie chart serves the function of communicating to the reader that all elements add up to 100%, but a text note or bar labeled "all other" can serve the same function within a bar graph.

However, area graphs are extremely useful in visualizing data with large differences in magnitude. Consider the following bar graph.

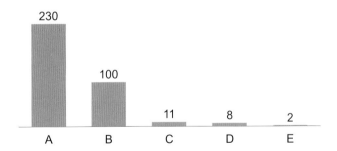

Figure 25. Bar graphs are poorly suited to large variations.

Notice how the bar chart is no longer an effective visual aid for comparing values across the graph.

Here's the same data illustrated with a tree map.

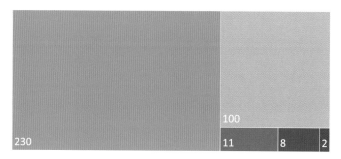

230   100   11   8   2

Figure 26. Area graphs allow better visual comparison for large variations.

Notice how the tree map, which uses two dimensions (height and width) to express magnitude, helps us to clearly visualize these large differences.

Circles are also commonly used in this way, as illustrated in the next figure.

Annual Revenue ($ million)

2018		2019
31		260
71		1250
8		360
25		210
38		150
173		2230

Figure 27. Use of circles in place of lines in a slope graph

If we had plotted this data with a slope graph, the lines would have been extremely steep and nearly impossible to differentiate at the endpoints.

Over the course of your career, you'll probably see quite a number of charts where circle area is used to represent a dimension. This visual works well for dimensions with large variations but poorly for dimensions with small variations, as our eyes have trouble perceiving the minute differences between two circles of similar size.

Churn rate over time

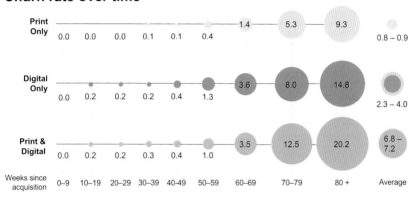

Figure 28. Circles are good for showing large growth.

Box Graphs

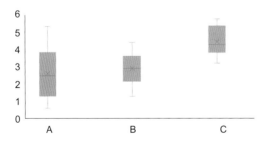

Figure 29. Example of a box graph

Also called box and whisker graphs, box graphs present bars with additional statistical markings, typically presenting the median and quartiles and possibly the **inter-quartile range** and outlier points. Box graphs are convenient ways to communicate statistics, but at this point you're already entering a gray area in terms of what your business audience may be comfortable processing.

Pareto Charts

The Pareto chart, although it's slightly specialized, is especially helpful for cutting through noise and highlighting the most important contributors toward business KPIs.

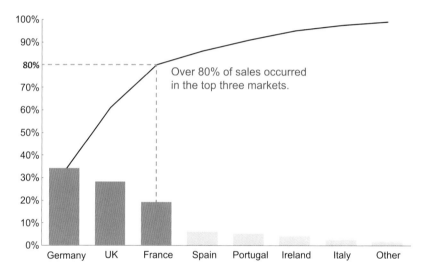

Figure 30. Example of a Pareto chart

Pareto charts use bars to show contributing factors from largest to smallest and overlay those bars with a line showing the cumulative contribution of the bars below the line to the total result. Because Pareto charts allow you to easily identify the top X factors making up Y percent of the results, they're a useful tool for helping executives focus their attention on the most important areas.

Extra credit: When you have time, look up "whale graphs."

Other Graphs

I've mentioned a few standard graphs that you can comfortably use with general audiences. Of course, there are dozens, if not hundreds, of other types of graphs, but many wouldn't be immediately intuitive to a nonspecialized audience. If you're communicating on a regular basis with the same audience, you may work with them to develop customized visualizations that are more complex but that communicate multiple insights to them using minimal space.

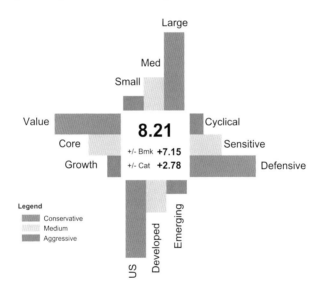

Figure 31. Example of a more complex chart tailored to a specific audience

An uninitiated audience may not understand such a chart, but for the stock traders with whom this analyst regularly worked, it provided a concise way to communicate on a regular basis the information they needed.

Insights from Graphs

The power of graphs lies in their ability to quickly give visual insights, but we don't know a priori which graph will provide the best insights. Sometimes you may need to try a few different graphs before detecting a pattern or trend.

Consider the following example, adapted from Stephen Few's *Show Me the Numbers*.

Job Satisfaction by Income, Education and Age

Income	College Degree		No College Degree	
	Under 50	50+	Under 50	50+
Up to $75k	42%	55%	41%	50%
Over $75k	53%	64%	60%	46%

Figure 32. Job satisfaction example in table format

Most likely, no insights will immediately jump out to you from this data table. Plotting this as a bar graph also does not present any immediate insights.

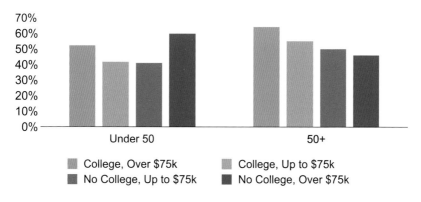

Figure 33. Job satisfaction table visualized as a bar graph

But see what happens when we plot this as a slope graph:

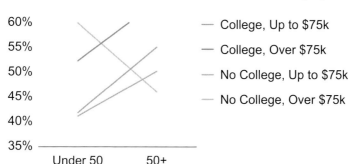

Figure 34. Job satisfaction table visualized as a slope graph

The slope graph immediately shows the only demographic that doesn't increase in satisfaction over time is *No College Over $75k*. This demonstrates how our choice of graph can impact not only how effectively we communicate our message, but also our ability to discover new insights.

Eliminating Clutter

Reducing Cognitive Load

How do we reduce cognitive load within a data visualization?

Start by eliminating everything that's not strictly nequired in communicating your message—unnecessary words or numbers, unneeded decimal points, repeated labels, lines, shapes, figures, etc. Anything that uses ink without providing value should go. Your new KPI should be "ink-to-insight ratio," with lower being better. Also remove any unnecessary variations in color, size or font.

In keeping with tradition, I'll quote Antoine de Saint-Exupery:

> *Perfection is finally attained*
> *not when there is no longer anything to add,*
> *but when there is no longer anything to take away.*

This wisdom applies to any element of any graph or table.

var A	var B	var C	var D
WW	XX	YY	ZZ
WW	XX	YY	ZZ
WW	XX	YY	ZZ
WW	XX	YY	ZZ

var A	var B	var C	var D
WW	XX	YY	ZZ
WW	XX	YY	ZZ
WW	XX	YY	ZZ
WW	XX	YY	ZZ

var A	var B	var C	var D
WW	XX	YY	ZZ
WW	XX	YY	ZZ
WW	XX	YY	ZZ
WW	XX	YY	ZZ

Figure 35. Tables with differing cognitive load

Many people feel more comfortable processing the tables with lighter borders, feeling that their eyes are freed to focus on the data itself.

Or consider the following line graph:

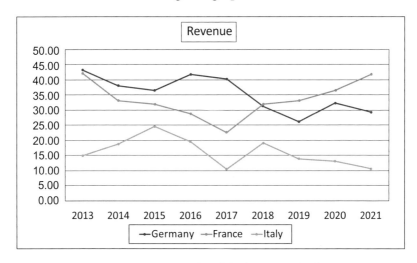

Figure 36. Line graph with high cognitive load

Do you feel how cluttered and heavy this is? The background lines distract from the data lines, and your eyes need to travel down to the country key at the bottom, then back up again.

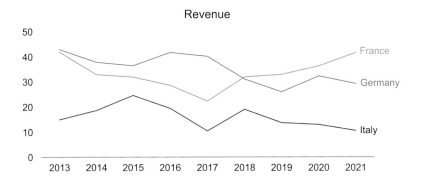

Figure 37. Line graph with lower cognitive load

You can see and probably feel the difference in this second graph. Your eyes are free to focus on the actual message of the graph.

But how can we data scientists learn to produce charts like the second line graph rather than that heavy first line graph? How can we systematically eliminate clutter from our own charts? One key is to visually communicate certain messages to our audience without even using ink. We do this using Gestalt principles.

Gestalt Principles

Gestalt principles, developed by psychologists in the 1920s, describe how our minds automatically identify patterns and groupings in what we see. Leveraging these principles allows us to remove any elements that explicitly make associations that are already communicated implicitly. I'll illustrate with examples as I present the various Gestalt principles.

Principle of Proximity

Consider these points:

Figure 38. Proximity implies groupings

Your mind automatically classifies the points into three groups based on proximity. It seems obvious in the above illustration, but consider this next one:

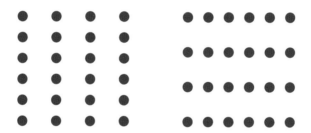

Figure 39. Table orientation implied by proximity

You automatically realize that the left chart should be read as columns and the right chart as rows. The proximity of the points communicates this directly to your subconscious. Pretty cool, no?

Why is this useful to us? I don't need to add visual elements for what my audience automatically realizes. In this example, I didn't need to add horizontal or vertical bars to indicate rows or columns. This meant I got by with less clutter in my chart.

Principle of Similarity

Likewise, our minds naturally associate items that look similar in some way—in color, shape, size, etc.

For example, our minds automatically form an association between the large circles in the next figure:

Figure 40. Similarity implies association

Similarity can be especially useful for communicating associations without clutter. Consider the following chart:

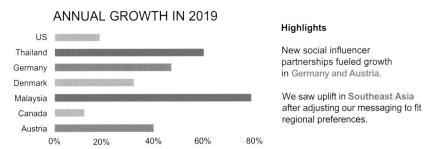

Figure 41. Text matched to graph by use of similar color

The similar colors communicate to the reader how the comments match the data bars.

Principle of Enclosure

We perceive objects as belonging together if they're enclosed within a common boundary. This works with borders and with shaded regions, as illustrated below:

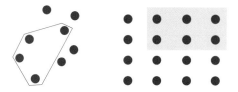

Figure 42. Example of points grouped by enclosure

To see this applied in a business context, consider the following table of financial results:

Region	Jan	Feb	Mar	Q1 Total	Apr	May	June	Q2 Total
North America	39,781	55,118	34,487	129,386	56,336	81,930	185,388	323,655
Central America	25,137	43,797	8,538	77,472	17,243	39,810	3,138	60,190
Australia	15,286	2,327	29,027	46,640	2,869	7,762	1,423	12,054
Europe	5,172	4,904	7,606	17,682	6,128	7,555	4,301	17,983
Middle East	30,943	853	25,539	57,335	35,933	37,379	22,618	95,930
South America	19,739	15,499	6,628	41,866	21,134	19,295	21,222	61,651
Total	$ 136,058	$ 122,497	$ 111,826	$ 370,382	$ 139,642	$ 193,730	$ 238,090	$ 571,463

Figure 43. Data table not utilizing enclosure

It's a bit difficult to separate the monthly figures from the quarterly totals, but notice how adding enclosure helps:

Region	Jan	Feb	Mar	Q1 Total	Apr	May	June	Q2 Total
North America	39,781	55,118	34,487	129,386	56,336	81,930	185,388	323,655
Central America	25,137	43,797	8,538	77,472	17,243	39,810	3,138	60,190
Australia	15,286	2,327	29,027	46,640	2,869	7,762	1,423	12,054
Europe	5,172	4,904	7,606	17,682	6,128	7,555	4,301	17,983
Middle East	30,943	853	25,539	57,335	35,933	37,379	22,618	95,930
South America	19,739	15,499	6,628	41,866	21,134	19,295	21,222	61,651
Total	$ 136,058	$ 122,497	$ 111,826	$ 370,382	$ 139,642	$ 193,730	$ 238,090	$ 571,463

Figure 44. Data table utilizing enclosure

By adding the gray boxes, I'm illustrating the Gestalt principles of both enclosure and similarity. Because of the principle of enclosure, the audience perceives that the quarterly summaries are distinct from the surrounding columns. Because of the principle of similarity, the audience perceives that the two shaded regions are associated. (In this case, they're both quarterly totals.) The end result is a table that's visually much easier to process.

Principle of Closure

Our minds tend to fill in gaps and close off open figures. Consider the logo for the World Wildlife Federation (WWF):

Figure 45. We view this open image as closed.

Our mind naturally fills in the missing lines around the head and back. This is the Gestalt principle of closure at work.

Because our minds naturally perceive objects as closed and complete, borders are generally unnecessary and are actually undesirable, as they raise our "ink-to-insight ratio." You may have noticed that most of the figures in this book don't include borders, although I make a few exceptions when I feel it necessary. Remove borders and you'll consistently produce cleaner visuals.

Principle of Continuity

Similar to closure, but slightly different, the principle of continuity describes how we tend to draw continuous lines in our minds. The principle of continuity is why we can get away with using dotted and dashed lines.

Consider the following example. We assume that pulling apart the elements of the first image will produce the second, rather than the third, image.

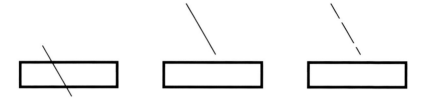

Figure 46. Example of the principle of continuity

Now consider the following chart:

Figure 47. The Gestalt principles of continuity and similarity are sending opposing messages in this example.

Do you feel a bit of mental conflict in deciding how to follow the gray line starting from the left or the blue line starting from the top? The Gestalt principles of continuity and similarity are sending conflicting messages regarding which way each line continues. This example illustrates the power of both principles.

How can this principle of continuity help declutter our visuals? Compare the following two bar graphs:

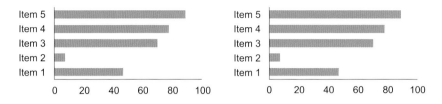

Figure 48. Subtle use of the principle of continuity in a graph

In the graph on the right, I've removed the y axis. Because of the Gestalt principle of continuity, we automatically draw that axis in our minds by continuing the left edge of the bars. It's a minor change, but it's one more way we've decluttered the chart. These minor changes will continue to add up.

Principle of Connection

We naturally perceive connected objects as belonging to the same group. This is why line charts are so powerful in communicating associations between points.

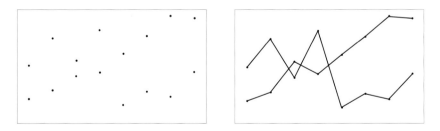

Figure 49. Example of the principle of connection

It's said that our minds view connection as a stronger signal of association than similarity or proximity, but less than enclosure. Have a look at the next figure and see if you'd agree.

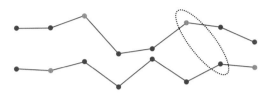

Figure 50. Connection communicates a stronger signal than similarity or proximity but is perceived as weaker than enclosure.

Example of Multiple Gestalt Principles at Work

Learn to use these six principles and you'll significantly decrease the clutter in your charts, freeing your audience to focus on the message you want to communicate. You'll often use several of them at once, and may even use all six within the same chart, as this next example illustrates.

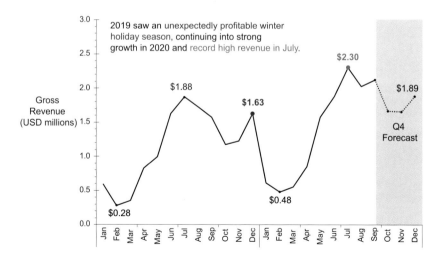

Figure 51. Illustration of six Gestalt principles within one chart

Take a minute to see if you can spot examples of each of those six Gestalt principles in this chart.

Focusing Attention

Remember that you need to make your point very quickly and clearly, because your audience may be extremely busy and unfamiliar with the subject. Your goal is to communicate insights with minimal cognitive load, and two of the ways you'll do this are by removing clutter and by adding elements that help focus the attention of your audience on your key message.

In the previous section, I explained how Gestalt principles help to remove clutter. They communicate associations without adding unnecessary ink. In the next section, I'll show how adding certain elements to a visual can focus attention and make your message stand out.

Creating Emphasis with Preattentive Attributes

I introduced nine preattentive attributes earlier in this chapter—length, width, size, orientation, shape, enclosure, hue, intensity and 2-D position. These attributes immediately stand out within a visual. Now I'll show you how to use preattentive attributes to highlight your main points and guide your audience as they scan for further details. This will further reduce the cognitive load of your visual.

To illustrate, if I want to make a point about Canada in the following bar graph, I can use a preattentive attribute to immediately focus attention on Canada.

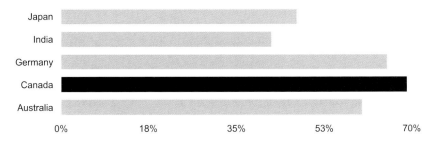

Figure 52. Focusing attention with a preattentive attribute

I used the attribute of intensity in this example, but I could also have used a different color with the same effect.

Using a preattentive attribute to draw attention to one visual element is simple and powerful, but you can also use preattentive attributes in more elaborate ways, such as to create a visual hierarchy within your visual.

Creating Visual Hierarchy with Preattentive Attributes

You can use preattentive attributes not just to make the main point of your slide or chart jump out immediately, but also to designate which other information is secondary, tertiary, etc. Your visual may contain a fair amount of information, but if you create descending levels of importance within the visual, your reader can decide how much information they want to harvest, based on their interest and available time.

Consider the following example of a report on missed revenue in the second quarter (Q2). First, I'll illustrate how you **don't** want to design a slide.

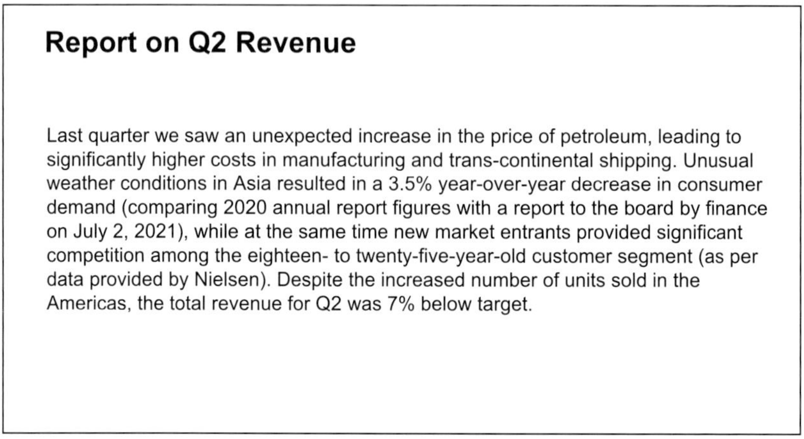

Report on Q2 Revenue

Last quarter we saw an unexpected increase in the price of petroleum, leading to significantly higher costs in manufacturing and trans-continental shipping. Unusual weather conditions in Asia resulted in a 3.5% year-over-year decrease in consumer demand (comparing 2020 annual report figures with a report to the board by finance on July 2, 2021), while at the same time new market entrants provided significant competition among the eighteen- to twenty-five-year-old customer segment (as per data provided by Nielsen). Despite the increased number of units sold in the Americas, the total revenue for Q2 was 7% below target.

Figure 53. A slide with uniform text takes time to process.

This slide doesn't meet our goal of quick and clear communication, because your reader will need to read every word on the slide to identify your intended message. This inflicts a heavy cognitive load and also leaves you as the author uncertain as to the message your audience will take from your slide.

Now I'll show how you can use preattentive attributes to guide your reader through the levels of information you want to communicate. Let's first look at these levels in your message.

1. Primary message: We missed our revenue target last quarter.

2. Second-level message: The causes were high production costs, low demand in Asia and new competition.

3. Third-level message: Details about the above three causes.

4. Fourth-level message: Technical details, such as dates and data sources.

You can communicate these message layers visually, as shown in the next figure.

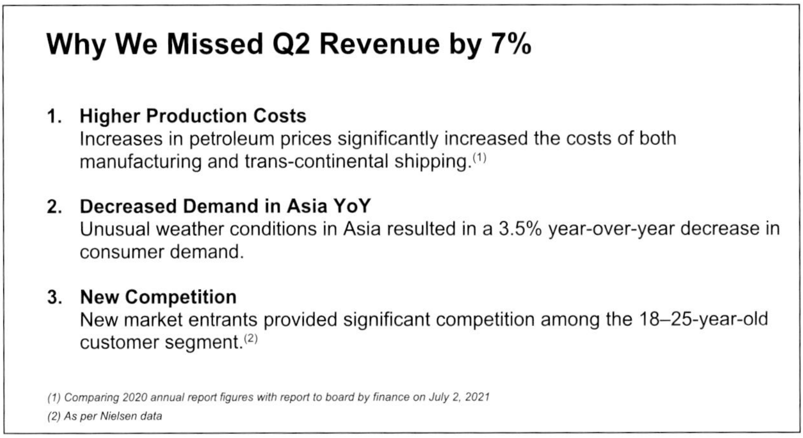

Why We Missed Q2 Revenue by 7%

1. **Higher Production Costs**
   Increases in petroleum prices significantly increased the costs of both manufacturing and trans-continental shipping.[1]

2. **Decreased Demand in Asia YoY**
   Unusual weather conditions in Asia resulted in a 3.5% year-over-year decrease in consumer demand.

3. **New Competition**
   New market entrants provided significant competition among the 18–25-year-old customer segment.[2]

(1) Comparing 2020 annual report figures with report to board by finance on July 2, 2021
(2) As per Nielsen data

Figure 54. Using visual hierarchy to make a slide user-friendly

The primary message stands out preattentively because it's the largest (size) and is positioned at the top of the page (2-D position). I've also made the title an actual takeaway message rather than simply a statement of topic, as in the previous slide.

The second-level insights (the three reasons) stand out next because they're bold (intensity), and stand alone on shorter lines (length).

The third level (the additional detail) is in normal style and font size, so the reader has the supporting information but could skip over it while scanning for main points.

The fourth level (footnotes) is deemphasized with a smaller font, light gray hue and placement at the bottom.

Creating this four-level visual hierarchy using preattentive attributes makes it very easy for your reader first to understand the importance of the various elements of your message, and then to make their own decision as to how much time and energy to devote to the details on the slide.

Notice how I didn't use color in this example. You might choose to use a color as part of the hierarchy, particularly to highlight key words or phrases to form an additional layer below the second level.

A Few Minor Principles to Keep in Mind

Here are a few principles that will help you keep your visuals clean and looking professional:

- **Leave plenty of white space, and preserve the page margins.** If you have more ink than white space, you may be trying to communicate too much on the slide.

- **Highlight sparingly.** You'll lose the effect if you highlight too many words using bold font or secondary colors.

- **Prefer simplicity.** Don't add unnecessary design elements, such as unnecessary variations in color or font. You can often communicate fully using only simple grayscale.

- **Use hybrid visuals.** Combine text, tables and graphs within a single visual when it helps make your point.

- **Avoid diagonal elements.** Diagonal connecting lines will make your page look messy.

- **Don't rotate text.** I mentioned this when discussing bar charts. Even a 45° text rotation can slow your readers down. A 90° rotation more so.

- **Don't center text.** You'll generally want to left- or right-align text to keep it looking neat.

I'll illustrate a few design missteps together in one example:

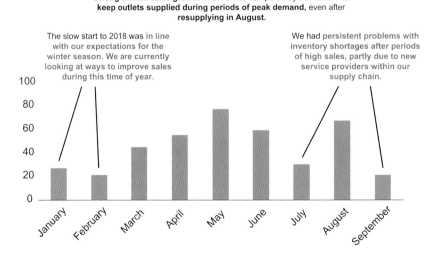

Figure 55. Design choices that inflict pain

That same graph looks much cleaner as:

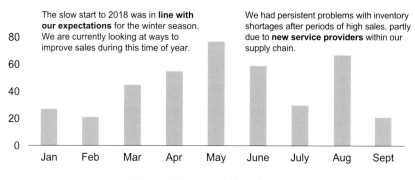

Strong annual sales growth in 2018 was hampered by our **failure to keep outlets supplied** during periods of peak demand, even after resupplying in August.

The slow start to 2018 was in **line with our expectations** for the winter season. We are currently looking at ways to improve sales during this time of year.

We had persistent problems with inventory shortages after periods of high sales, partly due to **new service providers** within our supply chain.

Figure 56. Improved chart design

Note how much cleaner this chart looks and how it communicates clearly even in grayscale.

Choosing Your Message

You've worked hard in the weeks and months leading up to your presentation. There's a lot you want to tell and quite a few charts you'd like to show.

Sadly, you'll need to leave most of your hard work out of your presentation. Choose your main point. Put the rest in the appendix. Bite the bullet.

I'll illustrate with the following chart, adapted from a similar one used by Avinash Kaushik to make the point in his blog, *Occam's Razor*.[16]

---

[16] Kaushik, A. (2017). It's not the ink, it's the think: 6 effective data visualization strategies. *Occam's Razor*. https://www.kaushik.net/avinash/its-not-the-ink-its-the-think-6-effective-data-visualization-rules/.

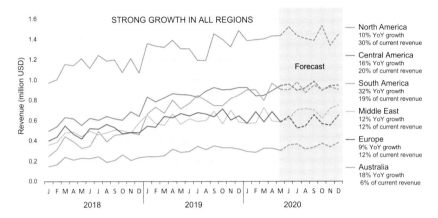

Figure 57. A visual with too many messages

This chart communicates quite a bit, especially when you look at the right-hand side. It communicates too much, in fact, resulting in no clear message. You can see how the author had so much to say that they couldn't hold back from saying it all.

So, what **was** the intended message of this chart?

Based on the title, the message is "Strong Growth in All Regions," but what does the chart actually show? Quite a lot:

1. Monthly fluctuations
2. Forecasts for the rest of the year
3. YoY numbers (that's "year-over-year")
4. Percent of total revenue in each region

What it **doesn't** do is what the title promises—make clear that there was strong growth in all regions. The data is there, but the audience is left to piece it together. Do all those monthly ups and downs add up to strong growth? Do the YoY numbers hidden on the right provide the proof? The audience won't be sure unless they focus and do their own analysis.

I see overloaded slides like this quite often in presentations. Because data scientists have access to so much data, they overwhelm and confuse their audiences by showing every detail, even when the key message is about a single aggregate metric. You should only show the fluctuations if your message is about the fluctuations.

What would be the simplest way to show growth across all categories in the previous slide? A simple bar or slope graph would do it.

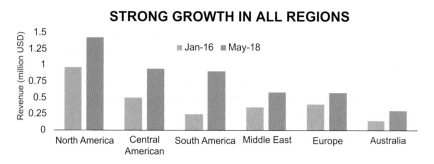

Figure 58. Telling a single message with a simple graph

You might want to add growth values next to each bar, but it's not strictly necessary to communicate the intended message. If you want to also communicate your FY17 forecasts, do that on a separate slide (with an appropriate title).

Live Presentations

Slides for live presentations should be constructed very differently from slides meant for distribution. In a live presentation, you need to keep the audience focused on you, not distracted by your slides. Your slides should help you make a point, at the very moment you yourself are making it.

Be especially careful not to display too much information on a slide. Don't fill slides with text or bullet points. Text-heavy slides generally don't capture people's attention. Also, don't display anything before you're talking about it. Your audience shouldn't be tempted to ignore you and read your slides instead! Worse still, don't find yourself in the situation where you stop engaging with your audience and simply read the slides to them.

Try to use a separate slide for each new piece of information. If you're discussing elements in sequence but need them to appear side-by-side as you discuss each one, use slide animation to build that slide as you talk through your message.

Slides for a live presentation should generally have one or more of the following three elements:

1. **One or more simple charts to illustrate your analysis.**
   If you watch the Hans Rosling statistics video I mentioned earlier, you'll see how he uses visuals to support the story as he tells it, but he never surrenders his audience to the visuals. You'll seldom show full tables in your presentations, as they invite distracted analysis rather than communicating insights. If you do need to include a table, add preattentive attributes to make the main point stand out. Tables usually go in the appendix so you can reference them during Q&A.

2. **A set of keywords, presented in a visually appealing way.**
   The keywords (often with icons) will serve as visual anchors to help the audience follow your storyline. The slides should not tell the story themselves. Again, never put yourself in the situation where you're simply reading slides to your audience.

   Tools such as MS PowerPoint can help you construct a more visually appealing presentation from a simple list of bullet points. In PowerPoint, select the "Design Ideas" item in the Design tab. Here's an example of what it suggested when I gave it a slide title and four bullet points.

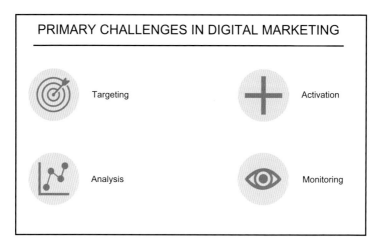

Figure 59. Visual automatically generated by PowerPoint

Again, the purpose of such a slide is to help your audience follow the structure of your message, but without distracting reading material.

3. **One or more large images to focus the attention of your audience on a topic.**
   Such "hero banners" help draw listeners into your presentation and demonstrate solidarity with your target audience. For example, you might display a picture of a freight truck when introducing analysis related to logistics. The slide decks I've seen within the fashion industry always include large product images, regardless of the message of the slide.

Your live presentations will benefit from intentional construction of simple slides, typically with minimal text. You'll be better able to maintain the attention of your audience and you'll force yourself to internalize your message rather than relying on text within the slides.

In Conclusion

As you pay more attention to the layout and messaging in your presentations, and as you grow more proficient in leveraging Gestalt principles (to remove clutter) and adding preattentive elements (to guide the focus of your audience), I'm confident that your presentations will improve significantly and your audiences will walk away with a much clearer understanding of your results.

Remember that presentations are an important part of your data science projects, as they're the moments when you showcase your hard work and solicit additional buy-in and support from your stakeholders. Your presentations are also the moments when you'll make memorable impressions on people with whom you may otherwise have little contact, such as managers of other departments and even senior executives. Making the most of these opportunities will pay off, not only in your current projects but also in your future career prospects.

Additional Reading

Stephen Few has written several books on data visualization. I've personally latched onto his thick hardcover *Show Me the Numbers,* which is filled with a combination of theory and practical tips.

Cole Knafflic's *Storytelling with Data* fuses some principles from Few's books with general principles for communication. She has recently followed this up with a book of exercises: *Storytelling with Data: Let's Practice!* The data and solution visuals for those exercises are available by following the links at www.storytelling-withdata.com/letspractice/downloads.

Adding inspiration from the broader data visualization community, Andy Kriebel and Eva Murray have taken what began as a community project and published a collection of principles and sample visualizations in their book *#MakeoverMonday: Improving How We Visualize and Analyze Data, One Chart at a Time.*

Few, S. (2004, 2012). *Show me the numbers* (1st & 2nd ed.). Analytics Press.

Knafflic, C. (2015). *Storytelling with data.* Wiley.

Knafflic, C. (2019). *Storytelling with data: Let's practice!* Wiley.

Kriebel, A., & Murray, E. (2018). *#MakeoverMonday: Improving how we visualize and analyze data, one chart at a time.* Wiley.

Expectations

CHAPTER EIGHT

Accepting New Projects

It's Monday morning, and the CTO calls you into their office. They're obviously very excited about something.

The first words out of their mouth are, "We need to build a recommender engine for our website."

As a data scientist, you're all in. You studied recommenders in your training, and several of your friends have worked on them at other companies.

So, what's your immediate response to the CTO?

"Let's do it!"?

No. Please don't say that. Not yet.

Step back from the precipice before taking your next step.

Instead of responding with "Let's do it!", the first words out of your mouth should probably be something like

> "A recommender engine. Sounds really interesting! There are just a few questions I'd like to ask …"

In this chapter and the next, I'll explain how to work with your manager, as well as other stakeholders, when given an assignment such as this. In particular, I'll cover the following techniques for stakeholder management:

1. What to discuss when you're first asked to take on a new project
2. How to conduct a kickoff meeting
3. How to communicate effectively throughout the project

This chapter covers the first technique. In it, I'll elaborate on a set of questions you should ask your manager right at the start of the project. Many data scientists, my younger self included, don't have the foresight to address these questions before they start on a project. Many don't even dare, fearing that the questions may come across as confrontational to their manager or stakeholder.

But asking the questions I'll discuss here will demonstrate to your manager the level of responsibility you're taking on with the project. More importantly, it will greatly increase the odds that your project will end in success rather than painful failure. And it may well be that, after discussing those questions in your first meeting, you and your manager will decide to not even undertake the project at all.

After I cover these initial questions in this chapter, I'll discuss in the next chapter the project kickoff, describing the why, how and who (participant list). I'll end that chapter by giving principles for managing ongoing communication with your manager so as to stay aligned and maintain their trust.

Note that in this chapter I'll refer to the person asking you to complete the project as "your manager," but this could also be a client or some other senior member of your organization.

Four Conversations to Have before You Accept the Mission

You should cover four general topics with your manager (the CTO in the example above) before committing to a new project. Address these at the start to save yourself unnecessary pain and frustration over the coming months. Trust me. I've been there.

These four conversations should cover

1. Situational diagnosis
2. Expectations

3. Communication style
4. Resources

Whether it's during a single meeting or over several consecutive meetings, having these four conversations will help clarify what you and your manager need to know and agree on before you proceed with the project. These conversations will help you uncover the real business needs behind your manager's enthusiasm and will lay the foundation for ongoing collaboration with your various stakeholders.

Listen intently to the answers your manager gives during this initial conversation and ask probing follow-up questions if anything is unclear. The world of data science is a graveyard of abandoned proofs of concept, each born in a conversation very much like the one you're having right now. Listening well at this point will be key to future project success.

Conversation 1: Situational Diagnosis

Your first goal is to understand the background behind this new data science idea. What has spurred your manager to bring this project up with you today?

Background

Ask your manager,

> *"What's brought this project to mind now?"*

Starting the conversation in this way will help bring you up to speed with the bigger picture around this new ask. In answering this question, it's likely that your manager will mention additional details that will be important for you to understand as you proceed to scope out the proposed project. In addition, when you understand what's motivating the request, you may be able to recommend a different, but better, solution to the underlying problem or opportunity.

Typically, the answer to this question will be one or more of the following:

- **Something significant just happened.**
  It may be that something just went wrong: someone missed an important target, or senior management is worried about something. Or it may be that your manager just received extra budget and would like to invest it in making an improvement they've had in mind for some time already.

- **Jumping on the bandwagon.**
  They won't say it in this way—nobody ever uses the word "bandwagon"—but you'll recognize this motivation when you hear reasons like "I read an article about this," or "I was at a conference and other people are doing this," or "we don't want to be left behind." Don't get me wrong. All of the lines above can be the start of meaningful motivations, but "everyone is doing it" should never be the basis for a project, nor does it provide a target KPI.

  I should confess that I've worked on projects where the stated goal was to find any possible applications of AI within the organization, and on projects where shareholder communication was perhaps slightly ahead of in-house progress. The important thing is to realize when the company's actual goal is "public bragging rights." Only if that is, in fact, the case can you justify pursuing initiatives that don't improve business KPIs.

- **Leadership wants to add a dimension to an existing project.**
  As part of business as usual, it's not uncommon for senior

management to brainstorm ways they can collaborate to improve KPIs. This is especially true for companies using **OKR** (Objectives and Key Results) frameworks, which call for high degrees of collaboration. In such cases, your manager may be offering your services to help another team or department obtain their objectives.

After this first question, you should have a basic understanding of why your manager thinks this project is important. At this moment, you should act as a thought partner, possibly suggesting alternative solutions to the problem/opportunity your manager has just described. Often, you won't be in a position to decline the project (e.g., if the stakeholder is your manager), but you should be able to challenge your manager's thinking and take and defend a well-thought-out position on the topic. A good manager will value this.

Whether you stay with the original proposal or perhaps move to an alternative solution, you should realize it's very likely that this is not the first time your organization has thought about projects to meet this stated goal. It's even possible that someone in your organization has already tried this specific project—and failed. Before starting your own work, you'll want to learn any history related to this request. If the project was previously considered or attempted, you'll want to understand why it wasn't completed.

With this in mind, ask your manager,

"What's the history behind this?"

In particular, you want to find out the following:

- **Has a project like this been tried in the past?** Are there people in your company who have worked on this or similar projects in the past? If so, you'll want to know what was accomplished and what lessons were learned. If such a project failed, why did it fail last time and what's different this time?

- **How did the organization get to this point?** If your goal is to fix a problem, is this a new problem, one that's slowly worsening, or one that's simply been deprioritized until now? This question should also give you an indication of prioritization, because persistent problems that have been deprioritized in the past are likely to meet the same fate in the future. In this case, take the assignment with a grain of salt, as it may be deprioritized again soon.

By this point, your manager should have already shared their own thoughts regarding how this challenge could be addressed. If not, you should ask directly.

Ask your manager,

"What do we already know about possible solutions?"

- **Have people already spoken with consultants or vendors about their solutions?** I've been involved in projects where this has happened, and no one bothered to tell me until the point where I started to present these off-the-shelf products as possible solutions. Not only did this waste my time, it also put me in the potentially awkward position of cold-calling a vendor who had already spoken with my colleague.

- **How are other organizations addressing this challenge?** OK, it'll be your responsibility to research this, but it's quite possible that your manager already has the answer. In particular, if your organization has close affiliates, they can be extremely useful sources of insights. When I led global analytics at the eBay Classifieds Group, I'd also hit up my colleagues at PayPal to hear about solutions they were using (at the time, PayPal was part of eBay Inc.). I also found connections I made at professional conferences to be very helpful. Learning from the experiences and expertise of others outside your department or organization can save you months of effort and alert you to potential pitfalls or dead ends you might otherwise stumble into.

At this point, you should have gained a fairly good understanding of how your manager is thinking about the challenge, including its current importance, its history and any potential solutions they may be aware of. The next thing is to start clarifying the project goals and identifying potential risks, possibly in ways that your manager hasn't yet carefully considered.

Goals

You've already asked why this project has become important, so you may have already spoken about the high-level business goals. If not, you want to make sure these goals are clear.

Ask your manager,

> *"What is the main pain point or business opportunity we want to address?"*

This is the high-level business question, framed in nonspecialized terminology. We're not yet specifying KPIs, so the answer might be "sell more products" rather than "increase click-through rate on the product listing page."

It's quite possible that your manager has thought of a project but hasn't clarified what the end goal is. This may be the case if the manager has just received unclear but negative feedback and is trying to address it. Or it may be that they've received extra budget and want to spend it on a pet initiative, despite not having a clear business goal in mind.

At this point, try to get a clear and compelling business goal. This goal will feed directly into your three-minute story (chapter six) and will feed into future executive summaries you'll produce for this project. If your manager struggles to provide a goal, try rephrasing the question, perhaps as *"How will we know if this project is successful?"* or *"How would this project contribute to the strategic goals of the organization?"*

If you don't have a convincing business goal, you'll get pushback when trying to drum up support from your RASCI team (described later in this chapter).

Risks

Almost every project has obstacles, but if **you** don't bring up the subject of potential risks, your manager probably won't either. Protect yourself by broaching the subject now, before you undertake the work.

Ask your manager,

> *"When you think about this project, is there anything that comes to mind that might present a risk to completing it, such as organizational roadblocks, resources or dependencies?"*

Talking about these risks now will help you determine where you may need to buffer in additional resources or delivery time, who or what will require extra caution, and for what deliverables you should avoid making commitments. You may already be able to start mitigating those risks in the upcoming conversation about resources. In addition, by asking your manager about risks now, you're laying the groundwork for your upcoming conversation about delivery timelines, as any risk they bring up now will impact those timelines.

Common Project Risks

Certain categories of risks will often be part of your data science projects. The following list is ordered according to most frequently cited in a selection of recent literature:[17]

- **Planning and Control:** Unrealistic time or cost estimates, scope creep, lack of project management.

- **Requirement Risk:** Unclear, changing, or missing requirements. This probably applies for every single data science project you'll do.

- **User Risk:** Lack of cooperation or commitment, unrealistic expectations, etc. Your manager will typically understand where this risk occurs better than you will.

- **Team Risk:** Lack of capacity or required skills, risk of capacity reassignment.

- **Organization:** Lack of senior support, subversion through office politics.

- **Complexity:** Use of new technology, inadequate security features, performance shortfalls.

In data science projects, I'd say complexity plays the greatest risk, since model fitting, training, and deployment are generally more innovative in data science than they are in traditional software projects. This innovation, coupled with frequent data roadblocks, increases the risk of project failure.

You might want to show the above list of risks to your manager and ask if they can think of any specific instances of these risks. You

---

[17] Arnuphaptrairong, T. (2011). Top ten lists of software project risks: Evidence from the literature survey. *Proceedings of the International MultiConference of Engineers and Computer Scientists, Hong Kong* (pp. 732-737). IAENG.

should be sure your manager understands that the project you're undertaking is indeed innovative and that it may not produce the desired results.

Specific Risks Relevant to the Project

If your manager is aware of specific risks for this project, you might hear any of the following:

- "We're planning a large system migration next quarter. You won't be able to work with the target system until the migration is done. Also, other departments will prioritize that deployment over their support for you."

- "You may find it difficult to orchestrate change within this organization or department. You should be aware that people will need a lot of convincing before they'll be willing to embrace this new project."

- "X wanted to do the project I'm giving you. They won't be happy that you're doing it instead of them."

- "We may have a budget/hiring freeze in a few weeks, so you may lose staff or not have budget to bring in additional support."

- "You'll need to work closely with X, whom many people have found to be difficult to work with."

- "Your predecessor in this role lost the trust of their colleagues. You'll need to work hard to earn it back."

Take note of these risks so you can again take them into account during the resourcing and timeline conversations that will be coming up.

Concluding Remarks Regarding the Background Conversation

After you've covered this first topic, situational diagnosis, you'll have a basic understanding of the project background, history, potential solutions, goals and risks. You should already be forming an opinion on whether the business goal seems appropriate, whether the proposed project seems to be the right solution, and whether the project has a good chance to succeed in its intended goal.

Quite often, you'll find there will be a viable solution that is less complicated than the proposed solution but that will meet 80% of the project goals with 20% of the effort and 10% of the risk. (Yes, you might even consider linear or logistic regression.) Or you may propose that an off-the-shelf or **AutoML** solution would give a quick win with minimal effort. Such basic solutions may not appeal to the data scientist in you, but they may buy you credibility by allowing you to deliver value and avoid the risk of future project failure. In such a situation, you'll pass on a cool project but will be able to spend the credibility you've earned when you propose a different, even cooler, data science project next month.

Quite often, you'll address risks and uncertainties by proposing a proof of concept or a **pilot** deployment. I'll talk about each of these in chapter eleven.

But let's return to the conversation with your manager as you wrap up the situational diagnosis, the first of the four conversations you'll have. At this point, you have a better understanding of the business challenge, but you haven't yet committed to anything. You haven't yet said, "OK, I'll get started," or given some other sign that you're planning to do the work.

Keep it this way for now. If you're out of time after the situational diagnosis conversation, tell your manager you still have a few more questions you'd like to go over, and then ask when you can schedule a follow-up meeting. You can't realistically commit to the project until you clarify your manager's expectations.

This brings us to the second conversation: expectations.

Conversation 2: Expectations

Since you and your manager may start with different assumptions of what "doing" this project means, the next step is to clarify expectations of:

1. What you'll deliver (broadly defined at this point)
2. When you'll deliver it
3. How you'll "keep score"
4. How the project will coordinate with upcoming calendar events
5. How it will be prioritized against other projects

Here again, it's very likely that your manager hasn't yet thought through these questions in detail, so you'll need to actively participate as a thought partner in this conversation.

The natural place to start the expectations conversation is by discussing what your manager is expecting to get at the end of the project.

End Result

Ask your manager,

> *"What do you picture as the end result of this project?"*

Of course there probably won't be a final "end result," as you'll continue developing and refining a useful product, but you want to understand your manager's initial vision for what the project will deliver. You might want to ask your manager about the following:

- **Functionality:** What functionality do we need? In the example of a recommender engine, would the engine produce product lists to be sent in batch emails? Would it be used to sort product listings or search results? Would it update in session for new visitors?

- **Repeatability:** Is the result a one-off analysis that can be delivered as an Excel file, or does it need to be version-controlled code meeting the department's standards for production code?

- **Interface:** Should this final product operate using an Excel interface? Can I deliver raw code or rather expose a **REST API**?

- **Documentation:** What corporate material will need to be produced related to it? Should it be documented centrally?

As with any **user story,** you won't iron out all of the details now, but you should start on the same page with your manager in terms of general direction.

KPIs/Definitions of Success

During the background conversation, you talked with your manager about why this project is important to the business, but you haven't yet specified how to measure whether you've met or exceeded your goals. Now ask your manager,

> *"What KPIs should we use to measure the success of this project?"*

It's easy to get lazy and not specify KPIs for a project, but remember the saying, "If you aren't keeping score, then you're just practicing."

You'll often have a primary KPI and one or more secondary KPIs. In the recommender engine example, your primary KPI might be click-through rate (CTR) on recommended items. Secondary KPIs might be number of items viewed before an add to cart, or returning visitor rate, or unsubscribe rates for recommender-fueled emails.

Your definition of success doesn't need to be a KPI. Success may simply mean meeting the request of a key stakeholder. For example, you may undertake a research project whose end deliverable is a board-level presentation. Success in this case may be that the presentation leads to approval for another project, or it may simply be that the target audience is satisfied with the presentation.

Timeline

The timeline discussion isn't strictly about deadlines. You certainly need to know if there are hard deadlines for the project, such as a product launch date, but you also want to understand if your manager has assumptions about how quickly the project will be finished or how much work is involved.

Ask your manager,

> "Would we expect this project to be finished by a
> certain date for any particular reason?"

You're trying to understand their assumption of how much effort is required as well as their sense of urgency.

At this point, you can frame effort in terms of T-shirt sizes—is this project a small, medium, large or XL amount of work? If your manager wrongly assumes that this is an easy project, now is your chance to explain the effort and uncertainty such a project would entail. In such cases, you could suggest alternative projects that would produce a part of the value but with significantly less effort.

Regarding urgency, it's possible that your manager is under intense pressure to deliver this project quickly, or that the project budget needs to be used before the end of the year. You'll want to know this now so you can pace yourself accordingly. On the other hand, the project might have a dependency that prevents it from being deployed for a half year or more. This brings me to the final point related to timeline.

You'll need to understand how your project fits in with other project milestones and calendar events. You'll often need to wait on the results of other work, such as front-end migrations, installations of new systems or on-boarding of new staff. You'll also need to work around code freezes, especially close to holiday periods.

Ask your manager:

"Is there something we need to consider about how the milestones and deliveries of this project will fit in with upcoming events and other projects?"

You'll get a more complete understanding of these dependencies later, during the kickoff meeting, but asking the question now will highlight such uncertainties and help alleviate any time constraints your manager may be tempted to impose on you at this stage.

Prioritization

Your manager may have just expressed a strong sense of urgency. Now it's time to tactfully administer a small dose of reality.

Ask your manager,

"How should we prioritize this project against projects X, Y and Z?"

It could be that your manager's enthusiasm for this new project has caused them to forget about the project that was top priority last week. If you're not careful to clarify priorities and manage expectations, you'll work yourself into an early grave trying to prioritize everything at once.

If you've worked with Scrum, you'll have practiced conversations that go something like,

"I'd be happy to do this new project of twenty-one story points next Sprint, so long as you understand that twenty-one story points of other projects won't get done."

Do the same with your new data science project.

"This recommender project sounds great. I expect we can do this if we delay delivery of the forecasting project by three months and stop doing ad-hoc analytics for the operations team. What do you think?"

You aren't turning down the new project. You're helping put it into perspective, preserving a work environment that will allow you and your team to deliver quality results for projects that have been intentionally prioritized.

Concluding Remarks Regarding the Expectations Conversation

Whereas the situational diagnosis conversation helped you manage the business challenge, the expectations conversation helps you manage your manager. This conversation serves partly to illuminate assumptions, partly to give you an opportunity to push back, and partly to force you both to think of details you may not have previously nailed down, such as choice of KPIs.

You don't want to start the project with differing but unspoken assumptions for the project deliverables, KPIs, timelines and prioritization. Otherwise, you may only come to realize such differences in expectations later, when you're already far along in the project. Such a miscommunication is generally bad not only for the project, but also for your career.

After these first two conversations—situational diagnosis and expectations—you should have a good basis for deciding if and how you'll proceed with the project. The next two conversations will focus on how you'll run that project—the resources you'll have available and how you'll maintain ongoing communication with your manager.

Conversation 3: Resources

By this point, you should have an idea as to what resources the project will require, including expense budget, staffing and deadlines. If you aren't able to get the resources you need, you'll need to push back on deadline and/or deliverable. But before you do that, here are some additional ways you can refine your understanding of what's needed.

Budget

Ask your manager,

> *"Is there budget available for this project, such as for software licenses, cloud technology, consultants, etc.?"*

It's very likely you'll want to leverage cloud technologies, especially to quickly scale up compute power or database resources. This would require a subscription to the cloud provider, and hence a credit card backed by a budget. You may also consider the build-or-buy question—which could lead to the purchase of an off-the-shelf solution.

If you're developing specialized tooling or algorithms for which you don't yet have in-house expertise, you'll probably want to bring in consultants who specialize in that solution. Although often quite expensive, such specialists may be essential in moving a project forward quickly.

Your manager may not understand why you might need external help. Explain to them the tradeoff between cost and time. Although costly, specialists may be able to complete a task in just a few weeks. Doing all the work in-house, on the other hand, may require you to wait weeks or months to secure internal resources, followed by another long period to bring those people up to speed with the necessary technology or algorithms, followed by several months while they make and repair the newbie mistakes that we all make when learning something new. This cumbersome process could translate into a delay of almost a year for your innovative project.

I'll talk more in later chapters about the challenges and possibilities with moving projects forward quickly, illustrating with a case study from one of my past projects.

Staff

The success of this project depends on the colleagues with whom you'll work. This isn't simply a question of negotiating the size of your team or the number of consultants you can bring in. Rather, it's specifying who within your organization must be involved in the project in some way.

I typically employ the RASCI mode for project roles (carried over from my eBay days), which specifies five types of involvement:

Responsible: Who is the single person responsible for executing the project? This is typically you.

Approver: The primary project stakeholder. This person defines the success metrics for the project and typically helps you, the responsible party, to secure resources and overcome roadblocks. The approver is typically your manager or budget holder.

Supporting: The people who deliver work. They'll be the ones taking tasks on your Scrum or Kanban boards.

Consulted: The domain experts. These people understand the data, processes, technologies, etc., and will make themselves available to answer questions as needed. They won't take on project tasks and will only attend project meetings as needed.

Informed: The people cc'd on demo invites, project updates, etc. This generally includes all other RASC members and probably also your stakeholder's manager, select representatives of units impacted by your project and any other senior managers who'll feel left out if not included.

The RASCI is generally formed as follows:

1. You and your stakeholder automatically fill the R and A roles.

2. You'll say what capabilities you need for the S and C roles. You and your stakeholder will come up with names or agree to contact the manager of an appropriate team.

3. Your stakeholder will add names of other managers who they think should be added to the Informed list.

Hopefully your stakeholder will then secure the agreement of those in the Supporting and Consulted roles, although you may take the initiative to do that yourself if you feel it's appropriate. Depending on the power distance culture in your organization, you may either approach the individuals directly or you may need to go through their manager. The culture may also require someone at the same or higher level of seniority to approach that manager.

Here's an example how I've gone about this process in the past.

I was launching a project I knew would require web analytics data, so I knew I'd need someone in the "Consulted" category who I could go to with questions about specific web analytics reports. Without access to such a person, I might misunderstand key aspects of the data.

As it happened, I had spoken several times with a web analyst named Sarah (because I made it a point to talk to people at the coffee machine and to generally be friendly with colleagues around me, as per chapters one and five). However, I wasn't certain how busy Sarah was or whether I could rely on her to respond to questions.

Right after I started this new project, I sent an email to Sarah's manager, Joseph, briefly describing the new project and asking Joseph if there was someone on his team who I could occasionally approach with brief questions. Joseph emailed me back, cc'ing Sarah, writing that Sarah could help, as long as it didn't require too much of her time.

That's it.

I can't emphasize enough how important it is to the success of your project that you identify and secure the support of the members of your RASCI at the start of the project. The alternative is to risk unexpected roadblocks midway.

For example, let's say your project starts with two months of analysis followed by some database tasks, but that the database team isn't ready or willing to help at that two-month point. In this scenario, your project is dead in the water and you've wasted two months.

Or if you're planning to deploy your project to production but no one from technology is on your Consulted or Informed list, you're probably in for a rude awakening when you get to the deployment stage and discover that your project doesn't meet requirements for production deployment.

In addition to securing the support you'll need to run the project to completion, the other reason for defining your RASCI at the beginning is that your RASCI will constitute the invite list for your project kickoff meeting, which I'll discuss in the next chapter.

Deadlines

In the expectations conversation, you and your manager already discussed hard or soft deadlines, along with a rough estimate of how much effort a project such as this should require. Now that you better understand the people and budget available, you can more realistically discuss how quickly you'll be able to deliver the project.

Ask your manager,

> *"Based on the priorities and resources we've discussed,*
> *where shall we set the delivery milestones for this project?"*

Sometimes less time is actually better. The longer you have, the greater the expectations. This can be dangerous, considering the high degree of uncertainty inherent in data science projects. More time between the start and end of the assignment also increases the risk that interest, prioritization or need for your project evaporate before the point of delivery. A long time period also increases the chance that something in your organization changes in a way that makes your initial solution no longer relevant (such as a change in strategy or enabling technology).

Regardless of how much time you're given to complete the project, you still want to deliver initial results quickly and continue to deliver incremental results, or at least reports, as per agile methodologies (more on this in chapter eleven).

Concluding Remarks Regarding the Resources Conversation

If you've made it through the resources conversation without hitting a roadblock, you should be ready to commence with the project. But remember that you still need to secure the support of the people you've identified for your RASCI. And as these people provide their input, additional complications or roadblocks may come to light, especially during the upcoming kickoff meeting.

And you have one more conversation to hold with your manager—communication style—in which you'll clarify how you'll work together during the course of the project.

Conversation 4: Communication Style

Your ongoing communication with your manager during the project is extremely important for a number of reasons:

1. **To ensure your efforts remain aligned with your manager's expectations.** The two of you may have miscommunicated when discussing your visions or expectations in a previous meeting, or your manager may have changed their mind or forgotten what they said earlier. Either way, regular communication will help you stay aligned.

2. **So your manager feels confident in your work.** Data scientists often spend a lot of time researching, cleaning data and trying techniques that don't always work. These tasks often translate into weeks or months between impactful deliveries. Regular meetings with your manager give you the chance to explain what you've been doing and to demonstrate your diligence and enthusiasm. This can go a long way in maintaining trust.

3. **So your manager can relay important information.** Your manager's seniority typically provides them with access to more detailed and diverse company news. If you're meeting regularly, it's much more likely they'll think to mention something that might have an impact on your project.

If you've worked with this manager or stakeholder extensively in the past, you're probably already familiar with their communication preferences. If not, you can take this opportunity to agree on the frequency, medium and content of your ongoing project communication, as well as to ask how deeply they'd like to be involved in the project details.

Frequency

Ask your manager,

> *"Shall we meet weekly so I can give you updates?"*

Your manager will probably be very busy, and you'll struggle to get time with them. Start by getting them to agree to a regular frequency (weekly or biweekly), then ask which specific day and time usually works for them. **Then send a recurring calendar invite for that time**.

Odds are that they'll frequently cancel your regular meetings. You can miss an occasional meeting, but if they cancel twice in a row, **reschedule the meeting for another time**. It's very important that you maintain regular contact with your project stakeholder. If not, the project may slide off track.

> *During one of my first consulting projects, my stakeholder kept canceling our meetings because of her travel obligations. I made the mistake of not rescheduling after her second cancellation and soon found that we'd disconnected in our views of where the project should be going. We never did manage to realign, and the project fizzled out before the end of the year.*

Medium

You may have your updates in person, over the phone or via email. Try to have them in person, as you're more likely to get a two-way flow of information. If your manager prefers email rather than in-person updates, ask for any feedback or updates from their side in writing.

Also, be aware that some stakeholders expect communication to come in the form of PowerPoint slides.

A client once asked me to give a project update during an upcoming video call. Her first question on the call was, "Where are your Power-Point slides?" (which I didn't have). From then onward, I made sure to always make PowerPoint slides for her, even if the slides just consisted of a few paragraphs of text copy-pasted into the company slide template.

Content

You'll want to understand what type of information is most interesting to your manager. Do they want to see technical details? Are they interested in team dynamics? Or do they only want to know that things are or aren't going according to plan?

It may be that you simply find out their preferences along the way. In your first meetings, you'll prepare a lot of details but only touch briefly on each topic. You'll take note as to which topics interest them and include more content on those topics in future updates.

Involvement

Ask your manager,

> "How involved would you like to be in the details of this project?"

Many managers have so much on their plates that they'd love to simply hand off the project and not think about it until it's finished.

Others may have a natural interest in the subject or the technology and be curious to hear detailed updates. Some will be obsessed with organizational politics and will want to be included any time other senior colleagues are involved.

I once worked with a manager who was new in his role and asked that I copy him on every single email I sent. That did feel a bit weird. An experienced manager will be strategic in choosing their involvement and may be explicit with you regarding what they want and expect.

In general, you'll also want to inform your manager when any of the following occur:

- You're requesting support from someone outside of your normal working group.

- A conflict arises and looks like it may escalate, particularly if it's with another department.

- A senior executive may attend an upcoming project meeting. (Hopefully you didn't invite this executive without your manager's knowledge, but this could happen if an attendee forwards your invite.)

- Delivery of a milestone is at risk (more on this later).

In Conclusion

A potential data science project will have a much higher chance of succeeding if you've thoroughly discussed key aspects of it with your manager or stakeholder at the start. In this chapter, I described four conversations to have before you agree to take the project on. One of these conversations involved determining the individuals who will play some role in your project (the RASCI).

The following diagram illustrates these four conversations, along with their components.

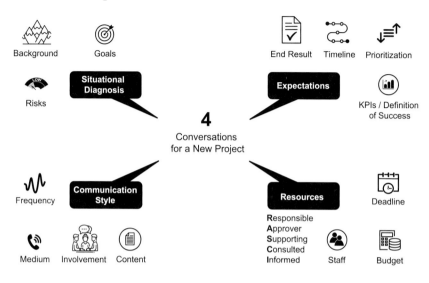

Figure 60. Topics to cover with your manager before starting a project

You may be able to cover all four of these conversations in one meeting, and most likely you'll start on at least the situational diagnosis and expectations conversations the moment your manager introduces their idea. Once you've covered all four, including identifying your RASCI, you can start planning the next key event—the kickoff meeting. I'll begin the next chapter with that topic.

Additional Reading

Watkins, M. D. (2013). *The first 90 days: Proven strategies for getting up to speed faster and smarter* (updated and expanded ed.). Harvard Business Review Press.

Patterson, K., Grenny, J., McMillan, R., & Switzler, A. (2012). *Crucial conversations: Tools for talking when stakes are high.* McGraw-Hill.

CHAPTER NINE

Building Consensus and Maintaining Trust

Your initial conversations with your manager or stakeholder helped you align on the most important elements of a potential project. But successfully delivering this project will depend on your ability to understand the perspectives and win the support of a broader group of individuals. It's critical that you start working with those colleagues very early in the project. You'll typically do this by organizing a project kickoff meeting.

The Project Kickoff Meeting

I know from experience how important it is to start projects by assembling all the right people in the same room to discuss challenges and proposed solutions.

The invite list should include everyone on the project RASCI and generally anyone with specific insights into possible obstacles or alternative solutions. If some of these people are unable to meet in person, have them call in or send proxies, but, either way, you absolutely need to start your project with a kickoff meeting.

The agenda for the project kickoff meeting is roughly as follows:

1. Review project background.

2. Present the proposed solution, including scope, timeline and RASCI.

3. Provide time for open discussion of any thoughts or concerns.

4. Agree on project rhythm going forward (frequency and nature of updates and any proposed changes to RASCI, particularly to the informed list).

I try to schedule one to two hours for the kickoff, but keep the meeting focused and flowing so as to cover the most important issues within that time.

Your own purpose for the project kickoff meeting goes beyond the published agenda. Here's how an effective kickoff meeting will benefit you:

- Preparation for the kickoff will force you to **clarify your own understanding** of the project background, goals, etc. You'll generally be able to reuse material you prepare now throughout the project.

- Attendance is a **first signal of whether members of your RASCI are on board**. If key members aren't participating, you'll need to flag this with your manager and consider whether you should continue to pursue their support, swap different people into their roles in the RASCI or perhaps rescope or even abandon the project altogether.

- This is the moment for anyone opposed to the project to **officially voice any objections**. You then discuss the opinions openly as a group and decide how to proceed. This conversation will help you later in the project, if you start to feel opposition from various corners, as you can reference the fact that there already was ample opportunity to object and debate during the kickoff meeting.

- It's quite possible that someone in the room will know a **reason why your project can't possibly work**. Someone may be aware of a law or contractual term impacting your idea, have a relevant customer insight, or remember a similar effort that failed for a specific reason. If there is such a reason, you really want to know it at the start of the project.

I'm sorry to say that I've personally had the sad experience of investing months into a data science project I'd accepted from a senior stakeholder, only to hear from an end user that the results weren't usable for a very basic reason.

- It's also possible that someone in the kickoff meeting will **propose a better solution**. This may be a much simpler solution, not involving machine learning, but just as effective. Again, you want to get that on the table sooner, rather than later.

Let me share an example of a project I witnessed where the data scientists obviously didn't benefit from the subject matter expertise that they should have gathered during a project kickoff meeting.

I once sat through a presentation in which two data scientists reported at length on a project they'd been working on over the past year. Their team was paying people to drive around the country recording images of street signs, and the data scientists were using computer vision to record the position and content of those signs. They went into detail about technical challenges, such as poor visibility. It was a large audience, and most attendees hadn't been involved at any stage of the project.

Toward the end of the presentation, someone raised his hand and asked, "Were you aware that there's a national database of where street signs have been placed?"

The data scientists both paused for a moment before one answered, "No."

It became immediately clear that they'd failed to talk to the relevant domain experts. This team of data scientists had spent months working on a completely unnecessary project, and it was obvious to the entire audience.

During the kickoff meeting, the input you receive and the discussions you have will be key in shaping your project road map. For this reason, it's critical that someone in your team take excellent meeting notes—who was invited, who attended, what was said by whom and any details that were or weren't agreed on.

After the meeting, write up the meeting notes and distribute them to all attendees, asking recipients to please respond if they see anything missing or incorrectly noted. Then publish the final meeting notes somewhere public, such as on the project's Confluence page.

Is everyone satisfied and agreed? Probably not. But at this point, everyone involved understands the project and has had a chance to express their opinions or concerns, all of which have been recorded. In addition, the scope and operating rhythms have been put down in black and white.

Now, if something goes very wrong or if someone on your RASCI later says they can't support the project, you can refer back to the fact that they had the chance to voice their concerns during the kickoff meeting. You're forcing them to keep a high level of transparency, and you'll do the same by publishing your notes, road maps and progress, using shared project management and documentation tools such as Confluence, SharePoint, Trello, Jira, etc.

Might there be changes to scope or timeline? Yes, and that will be reflected in further documentation (also posted in a shared location), but at least everyone starts out on the same page.

Ongoing Communication with Your Manager

Your ultimate goal is that your manager can give you an assignment and not have to think about it until it's finished or until you need their (infrequent) assistance. But how do you manage information flow to them while the project is underway?

Remember that senior managers have a lot to think about. Your goal is to make their job easier by convincing them that they only need to worry about the project when you tell them they need to worry. Your manager should never wonder if the project is going well. And if they happen to think of a good idea for the project, they should be confident that you've already explored the possibility.

In short, your manager should trust that you've taken complete ownership of the project, that you care about it more than they do and that you'll take the initiative to tell them if something isn't going well. Let me elaborate on that last point, as knowing when, and how, to bring up setbacks or bad news is a skill in itself.

Communicating When Things Aren't Going Well

When I give trainings on this topic, I always ask participants the question:

> True or False: "Don't communicate bad news until
> you're sure it's bad news."

I get mixed responses. It's a difficult question. We don't want to needlessly worry our manager, and yet all sorts of bad things can happen if we don't communicate problems promptly, before they become crises.

I typically continue by giving an example.

Your roommate's paycheck, which normally is deposited the first of each month, is two days late. The rent is due on the tenth. When do you expect your roommate to tell you they're not sure if they'll have money for the rent?

You'd probably like to know now, rather than next week, so you can start planning accordingly and thinking through possible ways to sort out the situation.

And what if they don't tell you until the day the rent is actually due?

First, you've lost options that would have been available earlier. Maybe you could have covered their rent if you hadn't bought a new laptop last week. Or you could have contacted your landlord together to explore options to postpone payment.

Second, you'll start worrying unnecessarily from now on. Every month, on the second day of the month, you'll ask your roommate if their paycheck has arrived. Why? Because you don't trust them to bring it up if you yourself don't ask.

You want to avoid a similar loss of trust at work. Rather, you want your manager to always think, "I know that project is going smoothly, because if it wasn't, David would have already told me about the problem."

Having the confidence of your manager doesn't mean there are never problems. It means that the manager doesn't need to worry whether you might be hiding them. To maintain that trust, you need to communicate when there's a realized or potential problem, even if you're still hopeful that the problem will resolve itself. This is best accomplished with a face-to-face meeting, if you can arrange one.

Your manager has given you ownership of the project. Don't use this occasion to attempt to give that ownership back. The purpose of this meeting with the manager isn't that they solve the problem for you. You're meeting them to do one or more of the following:

- Keep them informed
- Get their approval for your proposed solution
- Ask their help for specific solutions that are beyond your authority

Accomplishing these three objectives requires a plan. Before bringing up the problem, prepare for the discussion in the following ways:

1. **Be prepared to talk about the problem specifically.**
   If it's about missing a deadline, be prepared with exact details of what was to be delivered when, to whom it was promised, and what the updated estimate is. If it's an interpersonal conflict, have a record of email exchanges or meeting notes. If it's a problem with your data science model, write out what you expected to achieve, what you tried to do and why you think the approach failed.

2. **Prepare an ordered list of possible solutions.**
   You'll want to prepare a list of several alternative ways to handle the problem. Your manager may have access to additional information relevant to the situation, and such information may dictate which solutions are acceptable (increasing budget, pushing back delivery dates, switching vendors, moving staff, etc.). By preparing alternative solutions, you'll be able to quickly move through options as you get their input.

3. **Form well-grounded opinions.**
   You should do enough research to enable you to recommend solutions and to argue strongly in support of them. Although

cultures differ in whether vocalizing opinions to superiors is acceptable, if you've been given responsibility for a project, your manager will expect you to have sufficient insight to give an opinion, even if you must withhold it until explicitly asked.

I'll illustrate with an example from one of my past projects.

A client brought me in to establish a new data science department. My role was to construct the strategy and road map, start developing solutions, hire consultants for the short-term and help recruit permanent staff.

In the course of developing one of the first machine learning applications, I had coded up a proof of concept and thought it would be most efficient to bring in a consultant who could convert my mediocre code into production-quality code. We found a guy I'll call Peter. He worked for a company I trusted, he seemed smart, and he was proficient in this programming language. I gave Peter the draft code, introduced him to some colleagues, and explained the purpose and desired end product.

You know how it goes when you start a new project: the first week is meeting people, reading docs and getting access rights. The second and third weeks you're starting to work. In this case, by the fourth week Peter was supposed to show an increment, but he gave some reason why it wasn't done. I was busy doing other things and trusted he was working hard. Fifth week same story—the increment wasn't ready.

Now I'm five weeks in and am seriously starting to wonder about Peter, a consultant I'd recommended that my stakeholder bring in for the project. Peter was slowly whittling away at the project budget and was potentially delaying delivery. But I wasn't yet certain if there was really a problem with his work or if the two weeks of delay on the increment were legit.

At this point, I brought up the issue with my stakeholder. I explained the situation and told him what specific steps I was going to take. I said I would monitor Peter more closely, ask for daily progress reports and have a call with my contact at Peter's company.

Peter, despite being a very likable and intelligent person, turned out to suffer from untreated attention deficit disorder (ADD). He never did deliver results for that project. He wrote some nice snippets of code that didn't do what we needed them to do. It was a train wreck.

If I hadn't mentioned the problem with Peter to my stakeholder early, it's likely my stakeholder would have eventually heard about it from someone else in the company, at which point I would have had an even bigger trust problem on my hands. My speaking with the stakeholder increased his trust in me, and it gave him the insight he needed when deciding whether to approve the pending consultant invoice. In addition, telling him after five weeks rather than after three months helped prepare my stakeholder for the delay in project timeline that eventually resulted.

In the end, someone else finished the code; Peter got help with his ADD and went on to contribute positively at other companies; and my stakeholder never said anything negative about the whole incident.

> *(Incidentally, I know a number of data scientists who have told me they have ADD. As far as I've seen, they've done well at work once it's recognized and treated.)*

So realize that, yes, no one likes to report when something doesn't seem to be going well, but an honestly reported and successfully managed difficulty can go a long way in earning you the trust and respect of your stakeholders.

Asking for Help

We all get stuck from time to time. It happens when we aren't familiar with a new technology, technique, data source or business area. It happens when we don't have or can't access the resources we need.

Asking for help is a sign of maturity. Typical ways we do this include:

- Asking end users to help us understand use cases (how they'll use the model)

- Asking business experts to help us understand the meaning of database columns or anomalies in the data (such as why 10% of the rows have exactly the same strange value)

- Asking technical experts to help us get started with new technologies, systems or packages

- Asking colleagues with seniority to help us get permissions or prioritization

Not asking for help when you need it is bad for you and is infuriating for your manager—a lose/lose situation that will damage your career.

I learned this lesson when I saw one of my colleagues nearly fired for making this mistake. He was given responsibility for a complicated, client-facing task. He'd had some training in how to do it, but, even so, he still didn't quite understand the processes and analysis he was tasked with delivering. Rather than admitting this to his manager and asking for help, he simply kept doing his work badly. He nearly lost his job when his incompetence finally came to light—not because of the mistakes he had made but because the company had lost trust in his ability to ask for help and leverage the experience and resources of the team.

Even if you aren't making obvious or dire mistakes, not asking for support and input when you might benefit from it can be a serious waste of project time.

I once gave a technical task to a junior data scientist and recommended he speak to someone on another team about a package that would make the task much easier. Two days later, he was still working alone on a task that should have taken him two hours.

There's a common, and simple, technique that encourages data scientists to help each other by sharing insights into the best ways to perform tasks. It's called planning poker—a technique often used by Scrum teams of software developers. In it, the team together estimates how long a task should take, and if one member's estimate is unusually high, their teammates can explain how they think it can be done more quickly.

Of course, if asking for help matters, so does offering it—and ultimately finding a good balance between helping each other and taking responsibility for your own tasks.

Overcommunicate, Please

One way to keep your manager from wondering or worrying is to over-communicate about your project. This may sound contradictory—to relax their mind by flooding it with information—but it works if done properly. If you directly send them regular, concise updates and also make more detailed information about your process available to your RASCI, being transparent and consistent in your documentation, then your manager can choose how much to read and won't feel left in the dark.

In particular, you want to

- **Provide your manager with regular, concise progress summaries.** I wrote in chapter eight that you should schedule recurring weekly or biweekly meetings with your manager. You may also want to send regular email summaries. If you're using Scrum, you may already be producing regular summaries at the end of each Sprint.

- **Keep your manager abreast of how closely you're tracking to plan.** Best practice is to use small icons, such as stoplight colors, in your project update presentations. You'll typically send a page or section showing each project or task, along with some notes and a small icon indicating status.

  Colored circles work well for people who aren't colorblind: green when everything is going smoothly, yellow (amber) when there's a delay or risk and red when there's a significant problem or roadblock. These stoplight colors are another example of making presentations quickly digestible for busy executives. Because color is preattentive, the project status jumps out immediately, allowing the reader to instantly see which part of the presentation might warrant further attention.

For colorblind audiences, replace the stoplight circles with icons such as directional arrows or partially filled (Harvey) balls to communicate status. You can, of course, still color the icon with the corresponding stoplight color.

It may be tempting to show all tasks as green, but you'll instantly arouse suspicion this way. No experienced manager expects everything to be going smoothly. All green would imply dishonesty, ignorance or underambitious goal setting.

- **Provide optional details.** For whatever reason, your manager may want to dig into details from time to time. You'll increase their trust in you and in your work if you continually document the details of your project tasks and provide them with links to that documentation. The idea is not that you're creating extra documentation for them, but that you're giving them access to the artifacts you normally create as you work in a transparent manner.

  You'll often add some of these details as appendix slides in presentations. You'll add other details in shared locations (Confluence, OneDrive, Jira, etc.). With such tools, your manager can view your backlog and active tasks at any time. I personally work hard to make sure my teams continually scope their projects and document their progress on systems that our RASCI members can access. When secondary stakeholders ask (often slightly ignorant) questions during meetings, I'll nicely mention that their questions are answered in our public documentation.

Remember, if your manager ever asks you if everything is going OK with your project, it means you've been undercommunicating.

In Conclusion

In this chapter, I explained why a project kickoff meeting plays such a critical role in launching data science projects, and the benefits you'll reap if all ideas, discussions and decisions reached in that meeting are well documented.

I also discussed ways to communicate with your manager so as to build and maintain trust throughout the project. Losing trust midway can doom both your project and your future prospects with that manager.

This chapter has been primarily about launching and executing a project that someone else has asked you to do. In the next chapter, I'll talk about how to operate on a more senior level. I'll walk through the process of choosing data science projects that offer the highest potential to deliver value in your current business environment.

TOPIC FIVE

· · · ·

Results

CHAPTER TEN

Determining the Best Business Opportunities

If you're not building the right things, it doesn't matter how well you're building them. This chapter discusses how to take leadership in identifying which potential data science projects are most likely to benefit your company in its current situation.

Chapter one listed basic ways for data scientists to add business value—being a thought partner, winning trust, presenting results in an appropriate format, etc. This chapter is addressed to more senior data scientists, who can marshal stakeholders and take them through the process of identifying, planning and delivering a larger, possibly multiyear, data science project.

First, I need to make a confession. There's something I didn't tell you in chapter eight.

In my illustration of the excited stakeholder asking the data scientist to build a recommender engine, that data scientist was actually me, a few years ago. My failure to follow the advice I laid out in chapter eight led me through a bittersweet experience, reinforcing some of the principles I describe in this book.

I loved the recommender engine project. We ran with it for about a year, laid a strong foundation, brought in really talented staff and leveraged cool technology that made my friends jealous. After a year, I handed over the project to an internal team and wished them well as I went on to another project at another company.

You can imagine my heartbreak a few months later when I casually asked an old colleague how the KPIs for the recommender engine were progressing.

"We turned it off last month," he told me, a bit too matter-of-factly.

That was painful to hear. My really cool data science project had died an early death. I needed to understand why.

The truth is, I had already started to worry a half year earlier. We'd realized midway that some of our top business goals could be achieved to a large degree through small modifications in Elasticsearch (hence my insistence in chapter nine on getting everyone with good ideas into the project kickoff).

But what had really killed the project was the realization that a recommender engine didn't actually solve a business need for the company. We'd fallen into the trap of getting excited about a data science project before we'd identified our actual needs.

This chapter will help you avoid my mistake. I'll explain methodologies to help you identify and prioritize the data science projects that have the most promise of producing value in your organization.

I'll start with the importance of putting first things first in your data science road-mapping—determining the right problem before working on a solution. I'll then discuss the process of identifying and prioritizing potential data science projects.

Start with Business Needs

Putting first things first in a data science project means starting with business goals. After my recommender project fizzled out, I developed the Impact Areas for Analytics Framework illustrated in Figure 61 below. I use this now in my own consulting projects.

BUSINESS GOALS	DATA SCIENCE TECHNIQUE	DATA	TECH	STAFF

Figure 61. Impact Areas for Analytics Framework

As I sit down with colleagues and stakeholders to evaluate or draw up a road map for a (potential) project, we fill the framework in together from left to right. We start with the business goals, such as reducing cost from excess inventory, decreasing revenue loss from churn or decreasing customer support waiting times. Only when we have formulated a clear goal do we proceed to the next four columns.

It amazes me how often I've seen organizations launch a project simply because they want to use a certain data science technique they've heard about. At a conference I spoke at a few years ago, one of the other speakers, the CEO of a company in Southeast Asia, was bragging about the chatbot his company had built. During the Q&A, I asked what the business goal of that chatbot had been. He responded that there was no business goal. He simply wanted to have a chatbot.

Or course I have nothing against chatbots. But I would say that you should only build or buy one when there's an underlying business goal. For example, if you have a high volume of nearly identical customer requests and your value proposition doesn't involve personal service, then a chatbot could serve your business well. In other situations, such as answering complex or critical questions or servicing high-value clients, a chatbot would generally be the wrong solution.

Many companies actually skip both of the first two columns (business goals and data science techniques) and jump straight to acquiring data, technology or staff. These are the companies that purchase or license the newest big data systems and start consolidating all their data into a massive data lake. Although they plan multiyear data migration road maps and bring in expensive data engineers, these companies often haven't yet identified **how** they'll use this data (the techniques), nor **why** (the business goals).

And many companies jump straight to the last column (staff), hiring data scientists before they know what those data scientists will be doing. These new employees quickly grow bored and frustrated by the lack of direction and may leave within a few months. What's worse is the frustration of specialists recruited for skills that the job posting said were required but for which the company has no actual use.

So, put first things first and start by identifying the most important business goals in your organization. If your project isn't tied to a clear business goal, it doesn't matter what staff, tech, data or cool technique you're using. The effort will get deprioritized, you'll lose executive sponsorship, and no one will help you overcome the various road-blocks your project will inevitably encounter.

But how do we identify the most important business goals to pursue? There are two guiding principles:

1. **Alignment**. Choose business goals that are aligned with your organization's core business model and current priorities.

2. **Teamwork**. Work together with your customers and colleagues to identify the projects in which you're most likely to succeed in delivering value.

I'll discuss each of these in turn.

Align with Your Organization's Goals

To align with your organization's goals, you'll want to understand the business model as well as the current priorities—which may change at any time.

Business Model

A business model is a high-level description of how your organization brings value to customers and makes a profit in the process. An organization's business model may or may not be obvious.

It may take some effort to identify the various aspects of your business model. Talk to colleagues; read through company reports. In particular, identify the most important customer categories, products and revenue streams, and remember that "importance" is often measured in terms of revenue, but sometimes in terms of growth or even some humanitarian purpose behind the organization. The latter is particularly the case for nonprofit organizations.

It's possible that your organization has documented its business model using Strategyzer's Business Model Canvas (BMC), in which case you can read the business model directly from that canvas. The

BMC was developed at the University of Lausanne in 2005 and has since been used extensively by organizations around the world. I'll provide a reference for the BMC at the end of this chapter.

I'll illustrate a basic business model.

Imagine you work for a newspaper like *The New York Times*. The business model could be that the newspaper produces content (news, editorials, lifestyle, etc.) and sells that content either on demand or by subscription. The model could also be that it offers content for free and generates revenue from advertisers and paid listings (e.g., classified ads). The business model would also incorporate delivery channels (website, apps, print), content sources, etc.

If you as a data scientist were working for such a newspaper, you might learn that the business model involved a significant revenue stream coming from pay-per-click (PPC) advertisements within online content. Knowing this, you'd consider projects with the business goal of increasing traffic to pages displaying PPC ads.

Current Priorities

At a high level, your projects will target KPIs falling into one of four categories:

1. Increasing revenue
2. Decreasing cost
3. Increasing market share
4. Decreasing risk

Although all of these KPI categories are important for any organization, they generally won't be prioritized equally. Financial organizations generally prioritize risk KPIs, whereas startups prioritize growth KPIs. Online companies will generally place less priority on cost reduction than will companies in the fast-moving consumer goods (FMCG) sector.

But your leadership may, at any point, suddenly change priorities. They may be facing revenue pressure due to a shift in the economic climate, motivating them to cut costs where possible. Or the emergence of a new competitor may make customer retention the highest priority. Or perhaps your company just received a large influx of cash from an investment round, in which case the new priority may be to scale up quickly, possibly moving into new markets.

In all of these cases, the business model hasn't changed, but the priorities and goals have. You'll need to align yourself with these new priorities if you want to continue to provide the best business value and retain leadership's support for your data science projects.

If you're in a high-growth stage, you probably shouldn't be launching data science initiatives focused on cutting costs. But if your organization suddenly comes under revenue pressure, you might want to pause the project focused on growing market share and find another project with more short-term financial benefit, whether it be by increasing revenue or by reducing costs.

Your senior leadership will set current priorities and may even request specific data science projects, but to identify the projects with dpoint of deployment, you'll also need to collect input from customers and colleagues.

Teamwork: Get Input When Choosing Projects

You'll need two categories of input: input for identifying projects that meet real business needs and input for determining which projects are feasible within your organization now. The first place you'll look to identify business needs will be your end users.

Involve Your End Users

You want to choose projects that match actual needs with possible data science solutions, so work directly with your end users as you scope the project. They're best placed to tell you about the actual needs. If you wait until the end, you may have already built something that doesn't help them.

In using the term "end user," I'm referring to the people who'll be using or benefiting from your project. If your end user is a customer, such as a shopper on an ecommerce site, you may be able to sit down with a panel of customers, but it's more likely that you as a data scientist will work with customer specialists within your organization—perhaps a dedicated customer insights team or colleagues with extensive experience in some customer-facing role. However, your end user will often be another department within your own organization. For example, you may do a forecasting project for the finance department or a cost-cutting project for an operational department.

In any case, your goal is to understand your end user's needs—alleviating pain points they struggle with or creating tools to facilitate difficult tasks. They'll have both explicit and latent needs, so when you speak with them—ideally face to face—you'll need to patiently ask questions to draw out their thoughts. Here I'm returning to the theme of empathy, which I highlighted at the start of the book. To be truly empathetic, you need to listen.

> *The recommender engine project solved a problem that **we** wanted to solve, but not one that would have most benefited our end users. We knew that the product we were selling represented a major purchase for our customers, so they spent weeks or even months considering their purchase. What we **hadn't** recognized was that our customers were*

willing to spend a lot of time browsing and comparing options, if only they could eventually find something they were happy with. The time it took to search for products on our site was not the customers' biggest pain point. The pain point was that either we often didn't have the products for which they were looking or the products we did have were not presented in a way that appealed to the customers.

And so, as we eventually realized, our customers didn't actually want or need a recommender engine.

If we'd started by empathizing with our customers rather than choosing a project we ourselves thought was valuable, we could have identified half a dozen better ways to help them while also contributing to our bottom line. For example, we might have instead chosen to develop a dynamic pricing project, with the goal of better matching supply and demand so as to maintain higher levels of inventory for our most in-demand products while simultaneously increasing the company's profit margins.

In practice, you'll often follow up on an initial discussion with an end user by scheduling a workshop with a larger group. In such a workshop, you'll further identify key pain points and opportunities, brainstorm possible products or projects and refine those ideas into the most promising possibilities.

After you've identified data science projects with the highest potential to help your end users, you'll evaluate the projects from the perspective of how they align with your organization's goals and priorities. Keep the projects that are best aligned.

Once this is done, it's time to get input from more colleagues.

Involve Your Colleagues

I described in chapter eight the process of bringing your colleagues together for a kickoff meeting. In that meeting, you encourage them to voice any ideas, objections and potential roadblocks. But the kickoff meeting takes place after you've already decided on a specific project. If someone in your kickoff meeting brings up a project-killing road-block or an idea for a completely different, but better, solution, you've wasted the time that you and your colleagues have invested up to that point. Worse, you may find it difficult to abandon an idea once you've come that far.

To avoid this situation, solicit your colleagues' input much earlier, when you're thinking through possible solutions to the needs your customers have expressed.

Which of your colleagues should you involve in the process of brainstorming and refining possible projects? Try to assemble what's known as a "T-shaped" group, where each participant has a broad understanding of your organization (the top of the T) as well as a detailed understanding of their unique domain (the stem of the T).

If you're developing analytic initiatives at the top level of the or-ganization, you'll want to involve participants who know your strategy and your technology, and you'll typically also select key participants representing marketing, sales, operations, finance, customer support, human resources, etc.

If you're developing initiatives at a department level (e.g., digital marketing, finance, operations, etc.), you'll construct the T-shaped team in a similar way, but with the T spanning the department, plus related technology (i.e., someone familiar with the relevant databases).

In either case, you as a senior data scientist will typically be the participant representing the range of possible data science solutions.

Depending on the project, you may also invite a colleague who's more specialized, such as an expert in NLP, image recognition, statistical modeling, etc.

I want to emphasize the importance of having a data expert in this group. In a 2017 global survey of data scientists conducted by Crowdflower,[18] respondents cited access to quality data as the number one roadblock they met in their work, with half of them ranking it within the top three obstacles to achieving their goals. This is why we want to take a good look at what data we do or could have available for each data science project.

The group in this meeting should be large enough to anticipate possible opportunities and hindrances, but not so large as to discourage individual contributions. I'd suggest including four to eight individuals in addition to yourself. Schedule at least two hours for this meeting, and have the group meet in person if at all possible.

A Note on Canvases

When I hold team brainstorming meetings, such as those described above, I may use one or more canvases to help guide the discussions. If you're not familiar with canvases, they are visual tools for describing, assessing or planning around a concept. A canvas is typically a single page consisting of a combination of text, images and blank spaces. Popular examples include Strategyzer's Business Model and Value Proposition Canvases. Many of these canvases can be downloaded for free from various sites.

Before a brainstorming meeting, I'll hang a large printout of the canvas centrally in the meeting room. During the meeting, we write comments and ideas on colored stickies and place them on the canvas. It feels a bit like we're back in elementary school, but it works.

---

[18] Crowdflower. (2017). *2017 Data Scientist Report.*

Case Study

I'll close with an illustration of the scoping process I've described in this chapter.

Imagine you're working as a data scientist for Airbnb, HomeAway or a similar vacation rental company.

Your business model includes at least two distinct categories of customers:

- Property owners who list their properties for rent
- Vacationers who are looking to rent a property

You'll want to explore possible projects for both categories, but in this example, I'll illustrate using the property owners.

How do we involve the property owners in the process of identifying what projects would bring the most business benefit? It's possible that your company has already established property owner focus groups that meet regularly. Or perhaps you have a list of owners who have agreed to provide regular input regarding product development. What's more likely is that your company has a department whose purpose is to market to and/or support property owners. Since your colleagues within this department will be in regular contact with individual property owners, you can work directly with those colleagues to understand the needs and pain points of the property owners.

As you sit with those customers or representative colleagues, you may get specific input such as:

- Owners find it difficult to determine what price to set for their rentals.

- Owners aren't sure if the description they've written or the pictures they've taken for the posting are as good as they should be.

- Some owners are disappointed that they get so few rentals from your site.

- Some vacationers require a lot of hand-holding, asking many questions before and during the stay. Many property owners find this burdensome.

- A few vacationers are bad apples, causing property damage or noise disturbances. Owners wish there was a way to rate the vacationers, similar to the way vacationers can rate properties.

You, in turn, will ask follow-up questions to make sure you understand the owners' perspectives in general and these statements in particular. You'll ask what solutions the owners would like to see developed. You'll propose a few possible solutions and note their responses.

You'll leave that meeting with a short list of ideas that you think could form the basis for valuable data science projects. These might include projects such as:

- An image classification algorithm that automatically scores the quality of property photos submitted to the site

- An NLP algorithm that checks for completeness and quality of text descriptions

- A chatbot that can serve as the first line of defense against high-maintenance vacationers

- An algorithm that modifies the price or findability of properties to increase the likelihood that each owner has a minimum number of rentals per year

You'll evaluate these potential projects against business metrics and priorities. You may decide that the chatbot is potentially nice for the customer but carries with it either too much reputational risk for your company or not enough potential to increase revenue. You discard the chatbot but keep the other ideas on your list.

Next, you'll involve your colleagues, the ones you think would be involved in or impacted by the projects you're still considering. In our case, the T-shaped group would include colleagues with specialized knowledge in:

- The processes and current best practices followed by property owners when listing properties and servicing vacationers.

- The customer's viewpoint. This may be the same person as before, or it may be someone in customer support rather than business development.

- Systems for entering and storing the relevant property data. This may mean bringing in both front-end and database colleagues.

- Your organization's current strategic priorities.

- Data science techniques that could address each issue (you and possibly an additional specialist).

Start this meeting by summarizing the input you've received from the property owners. This would feed into the business objectives column in the Impact Areas for Analytics Framework (Figure 61). Your proposed data science techniques will go into the second column in the corresponding row. Use this as the starting point for your discussion in the meeting. Participants then contribute their insights, concerns and proposals for each business objective and corresponding data science technique.

As you together converge on the data science projects that seem most promising from both a technical and business perspective, you can proceed to flesh out details related to supporting data, technology and staffing.

Toward the end of this meeting, you'll have a short list of high-potential, high-impact projects. Now you should form a (well-defended) opinion about which projects to undertake. Create a clear presentation that summarizes your insights and proposals and schedule a time to present it to your senior leadership.

In Conclusion

Set aside time with end users and key business colleagues to understand business needs, brainstorm possibilities and refine ideas. If you do this before you even decide which projects to undertake, you'll greatly improve the chance that you'll choose projects that both bring business value and have a high chance of success.

Involving your stakeholders at this early stage will also give them a greater attachment to the projects. If they see them as projects that they themselves helped to create, they'll be more likely to lend support over the course of the project. You'll need all the stakeholder support you can get along the long, winding road your project will travel from inception to deployment.

This brings us to the subject of our next chapter—the methodologies used to get data science projects done.

Additional Reading

Osterwalder, A., & Pigneur, Y. (2010). *Business model generation: A handbook for visionaries, game changers, and challengers.* John Wiley & Sons.

Osterwalder, A., Pigneur, Y., Bernarda, G., Smith, A., & Papadakos, P. (2015). *Value proposition design: How to create products and services customers want.* John Wiley & Sons.

Harvard Business Review, Brown, T., Christensen, C. M., Nooyi, I., & Govindarajan, V. (2020). *HBR's 10 must reads on design thinking (with featured article* "Design Thinking" *By Tim Brown).* Harvard Business Review Press.

CHAPTER ELEVEN

Getting Projects Done

The goal of this chapter is to help you understand principles, frameworks and tooling that will be extremely useful to you and your teams as you work to deliver projects. If you're not yet familiar with the basic terminology in this chapter (**MVP,** PoC, pilot, user story, etc.), please refer to the glossary at the end of this book.

I'll explain tools and concepts that will help you develop your ideas into fully functional products, navigating the complexities and uncertainties inherent in real-world applications of data science. But there's much about analytic work that you first need to unlearn.

Unlearning the Meaning of "Work Well Done"

Most of us who are employed as data scientists spent roughly twenty years working our way through the educational system. Those twenty years instilled in us some strong principles and habits, many of which we need to dismantle as we adapt to a business environment.

School, unlike the business world, gave us clearly defined problems—along with the data we'd need to solve them. When starting each problem, we'd typically have a good idea as to how difficult it should be. Most importantly, we only received full credit when our solutions were exactly correct. Perfection mattered more than speed or simplicity, so shortcuts and approximations were penalized.

In our professional roles as data scientists, none of this holds true anymore.

Few people in our organizations understand what we should be doing as data scientists. They can't assess how difficult our tasks are, and they often can't even tell if our solutions are correct. What's worse, people generally don't even care about the quality of our work in the same way that we do. They don't care if we tell them the F1 score improved by five percent.

But they do care if they perceive that what we've done over the past three weeks doesn't connect to their business goals.

If you're coming out of a PhD program (like I was), you're in an even more difficult situation. No one will value your ability to disappear into a small room for two years and emerge with an airtight mathematical proof. Unless you're working on an application with no room for error, such as self-driving cars, your colleagues are now expecting the kind of intuitive reasoning and not-quite-finished work that would have gotten you kicked out of school.

Unfortunately, you can't change organizational culture to match your personal standards or values. So, it's time to change your own definition of "work well done" to include delivering "good enough" solutions to the most important problems, within time frames that meet business needs and expectations.

Equally important to delivering "good enough" results is developing the ability to manage ambiguity.

Three Sources of Ambiguity You'll Need to Manage

Getting data science projects done will require you to manage three significant sources of ambiguity:

1. **Your problems aren't clearly defined.**
   Rather than beginning with a clear view of the end goal, you'll need to continually define and redefine your goals throughout the course of the project. Even fundamental

questions—target KPIs, the form of your deliverables, update frequency—may change over the course of development. This is partly because your stakeholder doesn't yet understand the project, partly because you don't yet understand the project and partly because the organization and business environment around you are evolving more rapidly than you're able to finish projects.

2. **You don't know when or even if you can solve problems.** You can check if others have solved similar problems (at other companies, for example), but your data is different, and your systems are probably different. If you're using new technology, languages, or packages, it could take much longer than planned to do the installation, integration, debugging, etc.

3. **You can't foresee every problem you'll encounter in deployment.** Getting the right answer in a test environment doesn't mean you've succeeded. Your training data might not match real-world conditions. A few years back, researchers at Google Brain developed an image detection algorithm that could spot signs of diabetes in the human retina with ninety percent accuracy. But the algorithm had been trained on high-quality scans, and when it was deployed to clinics in Thailand, the actual image quality significantly limited the effectiveness of the algorithm.[19] Similarly, your solution may have unexpected and undesirable results when deployed, such as revealing one customer's personal information to another or perhaps displaying digital advertisements at inappropriate places.

---

[19] https://www.technologyreview.com/2020/04/27/1000658/google-medical-ai-accurate-lab-real-life-clinic-covid-diabetes-retina-disease/, accessed Sept 4, 2020.

These are challenges you typically didn't face in your training, but they're each extremely important in your work now. To meet them, you need to make a fundamental change in how you work as a data scientist.

Overcoming These Three Sources of Ambiguity

In this section, I'll describe how data scientists can work to overcome these sources of ambiguity, each of which has the potential to derail your project. Along the way, I'll promote concepts and methodologies commonly used by software development teams.

First Challenge: Your Problems Are Not Clearly Defined

Remember, you shouldn't expect to be able to fully scope all requirements, solutions and delivery timelines at the start of a project. You'll always run into new challenges, whether they be unforeseen problems or unrealized or updated requirements. Your goal isn't to develop perfect scoping skills, it's to develop the ability to work closely with your colleagues, stakeholders and end users at every stage of the project. This will allow you to steer the project properly, despite an initial lack of clarity.

Are you someone who likes working alone and keeping to yourself? That needs to change. Constant communication is key to success now.

Establish and maintain close contact with your end users. Ask them which instant messaging channels they use and get on those channels so you can get quick input from them.

In many cases, you'll have scoped the problem out reasonably well at the beginning of the project and will have created or inherited a partially developed use case. A use case is, in principle, your problem definition, but remember that your problem may never be completely defined. Neither you nor your end user can possibly have thought through all aspects of the situation, or all of the potential roadblocks you might hit. So even if you think the problem is fully scoped, you still want to keep the communication flowing.

The user story, in contrast to the use case, is the high-level description that gets you pointed in the right direction. The user story is the way your end user will typically describe the project when not going into a lot of detail. If you start with a user story, rather than a complete use case, you and your end user will have the expectation that you'll continue working in close collaboration to flesh out additional details.

It's critical that you frequently update your end user about your progress. This regular conversation will be enlightening in several ways. Sometimes we're convinced we're on the right track, until the end user tells us it's not what they wanted. At other times we think we've fallen far short, yet the end user is happy with the results.

Working with minimum viable products (MVPs) is a great way for both you and your end user to get this level of clarification. The MVP serves several purposes in your project:

1. The MVP is something that can actually be used.

2. The MVP proves to your colleagues that you as a data scientist can create something useful. I'm not joking.

3. The MVP invites user feedback earlier rather than later.

Let me underscore this third point. We data scientists need to make this shift in mindset—delivering something half-baked, something that would have earned us a low grade in university, is OK now. In fact, it's necessary. We need to kill the old mindset of aiming for perfection, especially at the start of a project. The alternative is spending months developing perfect solutions for problems that weren't yet clearly defined (even if we'd thought they were). This is a sure recipe for failure.

Second Challenge: You Don't Know If Your Problem Is Solvable

"The journey of a thousand miles begins with a single step."

No. Wrong. As a data scientist, you don't want that quote on your office wall.

Your journey of a thousand miles needs to begin with a walk around the block—your proof of concept (PoC). The PoC may not actually take you anywhere you need to go, but when you're finished, you'll have a much better idea of whether or not you should start the real journey.

To continue with the travel metaphor, your PoC is where you kick the tires to see if they fall off. Explore the data, the connections, the modeling. This will be manual work with greatly reduced scope, but it is likely to reveal potential problems.

Data scientists love PoCs. They offer the opportunity to try new algorithms or software packages using imperfect data and without the need to integrate into production systems. However, although the highly innovative nature of data science requires data scientists to run more PoCs than their colleagues in IT or BI, you need to discipline yourself to balance the time you spend on PoCs with the time you spend developing MVPs, pilots and full deployments.

Be critical about which PoCs you undertake. Choose the ones that offer the most promise of producing business value, such as applications that have demonstrated value at other companies and about which your own end users are enthusiastic. And as you develop those POCs, be thinking about future MVPs and discussing potential pilots with your stakeholders.

Third Challenge: New Problems Will Surface during Deployment

Data science projects face a stream of uncertainties: Will data continue to be complete and accurate? Will the privacy officer approve your use of data? Will the end users accept the model results? Will the initial model be stable when retrained?

One of the most common challenges is that the data isn't what you were expecting or promised. You'll often discover that values are consistently missing or filled with default values. It could be that several systems that used different definitions were at one point merged but not reconciled. Data fields you're relying on may contain what seem to be significant errors. Hopefully you'll have realized many of these problems during the PoC, but the PoC only focuses on validating specific aspects of a proposed solution. It's not uncommon to assume other aspects of your solution will work seamlessly, only to be unpleasantly surprised later.

An MVP, being a functional deliverable, will force you to use data sources, libraries and connections sooner rather than later, helping to expose any unexpected omissions or unforeseen incompatibilities. When you discover an unexpected problem, you'll have time to fix it or plan a work-around then, rather than in the days immediately preceding a critical delivery.

I was recently leading a project in which our MVP revealed that key data, which we assumed was complete, had significant problems. Our product was scheduled to be used within a few months, but we knew that delivering an MVP ahead of time would increase the likelihood of producing a strong end deliverable. As we prepared the MVP, we realized that the load job for the data source we were using had filtered out roughly one-third of the data driving our model. We hadn't realized the data was missing until we were able to start benchmarking the output of our MVP against the output of other systems. We were fortunate we'd realized the problem earlier rather than later, thanks to having developed the MVP.

Some of the problems you'll encounter, such as missing training data, can be addressed before deployment, but some will only surface after deployment. This is the reason you should work with pilots, or limited scope deployments. Pilots have the following advantages over full-out deployments:

1. Choosing a less important or less risky area for your pilot minimizes damage if something goes wrong. For example, new functionality rolled out to a region with five thousand customers generally has less impact if it crashes than if it had been rolled out to a million customers.

2. It's often easier to get permission, buy-in or support for a pilot. For example, it could be that the country manager in Canada is excited about your tool. After a successful pilot in Canada, the other country managers may be more receptive to deployment in their regions.

3. Pilots provide an opportunity to load-test your application. Your model may work fine in testing but be slower or more memory-hungry than expected when run real-time in production. Running the pilot will help you better understand the model's ability to scale to full production.

It's very common to both develop an MVP and deploy your solution as a pilot. I'll illustrate how this proved extremely beneficial in one of my past projects.

I was once tasked with leading a demand forecasting project for a multinational organization. The dollar amounts at stake were quite large, and the end users for the project were not technical. The problem was technically very difficult, and the tool we were creating would potentially replace the work of internal experts.

We later discovered that several teams around the globe had been given a very similar assignment, but that none of the stakeholders were happy with results from those other teams. Not a surprise, as the use case was pretty much impossible. In fact, one of the teams had consulted a university researcher who had also told them that the project was analytically impossible. We found this all out later, after we'd started delivering results.

What we did differently in our approach to the problem was that we didn't try to solve the whole problem at once. Instead, we kept close communication with one particular end user (I'll call him Roger) who was especially excited about our project and was willing to give us the input we needed. We chose Roger's market as our pilot. Roger sat with us to explain the current business processes, the relative importance of the different product types, the pain points and the solutions he wanted to see.

We realized in talking with Roger that we could get a "quick win" by initially limiting our work to a certain subset of products. We also realized that Roger really just needed a very basic solution to make his life a hundred times easier.

As a data scientist with a PhD, leading a team of other PhDs, I swallowed my pride and started building a forecasting tool that was so incredibly basic that I was embarrassed to talk about it. This was going to be our MVP—the very first step in what (we expected) would grow to become a really cool, sophisticated forecasting tool.

To my surprise, Roger loved our MVP. In fact, everyone outside my team loved the MVP. We did iterate several times before the actual pilot forecast, but in the end, our deliverable used a painfully simple technique that could forecast demand for a limited set of products. Even though we data scientists had wanted to develop a better, more complete, and certainly more complicated solution, what we delivered for that pilot was what the end users wanted.

Our deliverable made a huge difference for the end users. We became known in the company as the only ones who were able to "solve" the demand forecasting problem. We were like rock stars in the company.

OK, not really like rock stars, but you get the point. Our end users were thrilled that we delivered what they considered to be a very useful product, even as other data science teams struggled—and failed—to deliver the 100% solution.

I write this to illustrate how PoCs, MVPs and pilots can be extremely useful to data scientists. Software developers also regularly work with these concepts in their projects, and you might argue that data scientists are following in the footsteps of software developers in this respect. In fact, software developers have developed a much broader foundation of techniques for getting their projects done—techniques that are generally proving to be very useful to data scientists.

Techniques from Software Development

Software developers have a lot in common with data scientists in that they also often work with ambiguous goals within a rapidly changing technological landscape. But the field of software development is more mature than that of data science. Over the past thirty years, software developers have been refining a number of concepts and methodologies that help them run projects in ambiguous and rapidly changing settings.

Data science, being a younger field, has benefited greatly by adopting many of these project management concepts and methodologies. However, data scientists have also come to realize that techniques that have proven so effective in software development may require some adaptation if they're to provide similar value in data science projects.

In this section, I'll look at the most commonly used concepts, frameworks and tools and show how we typically adapt them to work for data science. I'll start with frameworks for project management.

Project Management Frameworks

Software developers have, out of necessity, developed methods that allow them to thrive in rapidly changing environments. They've abandoned the traditional "Waterfall" methodology for project management in favor of what has become known as "Agile." Let's take a look at what this shift in methodologies means with regard to completing projects.

Waterfall Methodology

Some projects simply take a long time to complete. The Hoover Dam in Nevada took five years. The Three Gorges Dam in China, about five times larger, took seventeen years,[20] and the largest flood prevention system in the world, Holland's Delta Works, took an amazing forty-four years to complete.

It wasn't unusual for engineering projects of the last century to span years or even decades. Even as recently as the start of the 1990s, it would typically take six years to design a new car and possibly twenty or more years to deploy a new aerospace system. Around that

---

[20] https://en.wikipedia.org/wiki/Three_Gorges_Dam, referenced Sept 16, 2020.

time, industry experts estimated a typical software project took three years.[21]

In this environment, engineers would generally follow what is known as the "Waterfall" methodology. They'd fully specify a project before starting work and then build to those specifications. The project progressed in stages, handed from one team to the next (hence the waterfall analogy). As you can imagine, this worked well for large projects—such as building dams—where careful up-front planning would prevent costly errors a decade later.

However, as projects increasingly involved software engineering, and as the scope of software applications grew, software developers realized that they needed a new way to work. That's when the Agile methodology emerged.

Agile

Software developers of the twentieth century, who often designed components within larger engineering projects, inherited project management techniques from traditional engineers. But as they used Waterfall in their multiyear projects, they increasingly realized how unsuited it was to software development.

Why was this?

Hardware, operating systems, software and networking were all changing rapidly. Business models were evolving, and end users' understanding of what software could or should do was changing over periods of months, rather than years. Software users in 1998 would expect much more than they did in 1995.

Demand changed continually, and software developers could no longer afford to code in isolation for months at a time. In response,

---

[21] https://techbeacon.com/app-dev-testing/agility-beyond-history-legacy-agile-development, referenced Sept 4, 2020.

some developers actively began looking for better ways to run their projects.

By the 1990s, concepts of incremental improvements (build-measure-learn) and "Lean thinking" (including Kanban) had already been around for decades. But software developers were still missing something. In particular, they needed better ways to:

1. More quickly deliver usable software
2. Strengthen continuous feedback loops with end users

To this end, they began developing—and sharing—new ways to manage their software projects. They introduced Scrum, extreme programming, adaptive software development and other practices that would become collectively known as "Agile software development methods." These methods brought fundamental changes in how software developers worked in teams and how they interacted with end users throughout the project.

In February of 2001, seventeen leading software professionals assembled at a ski resort in Utah to share concerns and ideas for running projects. They condensed their conclusions into a set of core values for software development, emphasizing trust, respect and collaboration. The result was what is called the "Manifesto for Agile Software Development." Their manifesto was short (68 words), elaborated with twelve principles (another 182 words). This Agile Manifesto is considered the definitive statement of the Agile software development movement.

The Agile Manifesto promoted principles for efficient teamwork, frequent delivery and close collaboration with end users. You'll see how these principles play out in the Scrum framework, described next.

Scrum

Scrum is probably the most popular Agile methodology in use today. Because it's so common, I'll dedicate a few pages to describing it.

Scrum (short for "Scrummage") is actually a rugby term. This sports imagery was picked up and developed for industry according to the following timeline:

- **1986:** Takeuchi and Nonaka introduced the term in a paper published in the Harvard Business Review, arguing that small, cross-functional teams historically produce the best results.[22]

- **1993–1995:** Jeff Sutherland and Ken Schwaber developed a framework for software development, based on Takeuchi's and Nonaka's Scrum model.

- **1995:** Sutherland and Schwaber presented their Scrum framework to the development community.

- **2001:** Sutherland, Schwaber and fifteen others composed the Agile Manifesto.

- **2002+:** Sutherland and Schwaber developed the Scrum Alliance, Scrum Inc., Scrum.org, etc.

Note that Scrum is a framework. You can think of it like this: Scrum provides the plumbing and the electric outlets, but it lets you decide how to design the kitchen. More specifically, Scrum defines events, roles and "artifacts" (documents or deliverables), but gives each team the flexibility to decide for itself what setup works best for that team. For example, the team can decide its cadence for delivering

---

[22] Takeuchi, H., & Nonaka, I. (1986, January). The new new product development game. *Harvard Business Review.*

intermediate results. The advantage is that data scientists can implement Scrum differently than software developers. I'll come back to this later in the chapter.

The core concept of Scrum is that, for development of new, complex products, the best results occur when teams

- Are small and self-organizing. That is, teams are given objectives rather than specific assignments and have the freedom to determine the best ways to meet those objectives.

- Are cross-functional.

- Work in time-boxed, iterative development cycles, with the goal of delivering working software.

The last point, "time-boxing," plays a prominent role in Scrum, more so than in other project management frameworks. But does your work as a data scientist really fit nicely within specified time periods? I'll come back to this question later. I'll first describe how Scrum works in practice.

Scrum has three roles, three artifacts and five mandatory events.

Because of the circular nature of the definitions that follow, I'll start by defining the term *Sprint*, which is the period of time (usually two to four weeks) during which the team focuses on project tasks. With that term introduced, I'll move to Scrum's three roles.

Three Roles within Scrum

- The **Development Team** consists of the professionals developing the product. They represent a single, cross-functional team with no subteams and no internal titles.

- The **Product Owner** is the person responsible for maximizing the business value produced by the development team.

- The **Scrum Master** is the individual tasked with promoting and supporting the Scrum process, working with the product owner, the development team and even colleagues outside the Scrum team to help keep things working properly.

Three Artifacts within Scrum

- The **Product Backlog** consists of the features or tasks that have been requested.

- The **Sprint Backlog** consists of the items from the product backlog that have been selected for the current Sprint.

- The **Increment (Sprint Goal)** is the delivery at the end of the current Sprint.

Five Mandatory Events within Scrum (in Order of Occurrence)

- In the **Sprint Planning**, the team agrees which items from the product backlog to put on the next Sprint Backlog.

- The **Sprint** is the development period, typically between two and four weeks.

- The **Daily Scrum/Standup** is a short team status meeting (e.g., short enough to stay standing).

- In the **Sprint Demo/Review**, the team and stakeholders together discuss what was done in the completed Sprint.

- In the **Sprint Retrospective**, the team takes an hour or two for introspection—discussing what did or didn't go well in the last Sprint and planning adjustments to improve how they work together in future Sprints.

You're free to add artifacts (such as burndown charts) or events (such as refinement meetings). That's the beauty of working with a framework—it gives you flexibility to do what works for you.

When you as a data scientist join an existing Scrum team, you'll quickly learn how your new team has implemented Scrum. Within a few weeks, at your first Sprint retrospective, you'll have a chance to give your input and suggest changes in how your team implements Scrum during future Sprints.

Although Scrum is perhaps the project management framework most commonly used by data science teams, it's not the only one.

Kanban

Many teams choose to manage their projects using the Kanban framework rather than Scrum. Kanban actually predates Scrum by about fifty years, having its origins in the Lean manufacturing principles developed in the 1940s.

Kanban is a workflow management system emphasizing visual placement of tasks on a board called the *Kanban Board*—Kanban is Japanese for "billboard." A Kanban Board will have several columns indicating task status (e.g., ready for development, in progress, awaiting review, done). Teams will typically place limits on the number of items allowed in a column at any one time, thus reducing multitasking.

Data scientists may choose Kanban over Scrum because Kanban doesn't require the extensive time-boxing that permeates Scrum and because it offers the flexibility to accept new tasks or deliver results at any moment, not simply between Sprints. I'll come back to this when I discuss "Scrumban."

Which Project Management Frameworks Do Most DS Teams Use?

Software professionals have poured an incredible amount of time into developing project management frameworks. We as data scientists should also carefully consider how we can best manage our projects— how we'll work as a team, how we'll interact with our end users and how we'll schedule the tasks required to carry our data science projects from ideation to production.

As we'll see next, different data science teams choose different methodologies, often changing from one to another as they discover what does or doesn't work for them.

In the 2018 study I mentioned in chapter one, O'Reilly[23] asked over 11,000 data scientists[24] which methodology they were using. Responses, shown below, show a heavy preference for Scrum.[25]

Figure 62. Most commonly used methodologies for machine learning projects

Segmenting responses by the organizations' stage of ML adoption shows a trend in which companies first move from no methodology category to Scrum and then on to the "Other" category.

---

[23] Lorica & Nathan, *The state of machine learning adoption in the enterprise.*

[24] Survey respondents included those who had attended one of the company's Strata Data or AI Conferences or had accessed O'Reilly content that covered "related topics."

[25] The survey actually uses the term "Agile," which I've replaced with "Scrum," since, per the May 2016 HBR article "Embracing Agile," Scrum and its derivatives are employed at least five times as often as other Agile practices.

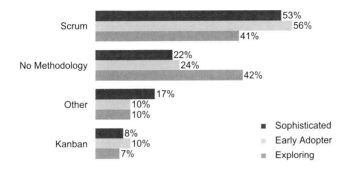

Figure 63. Project methodology split by ML maturity

I've seen this progression myself, where data science teams try using Scrum but eventually develop a hybrid approach that they feel is better suited to the more uncertain tasks and sometimes less stringent deadlines of their work. Let's look at one of the more popular hybridizations—one I often use in my own projects.

Scrumban

Scrumban, which I briefly referenced earlier, mixes elements from both Scrum and Kanban. I've often found myself drifting from Scrum to Scrumban over the course of a data science project. In such cases, I typically end up using the roles and events of Scrum but relaxing Scrum's time-boxing requirements and allowing mid-Sprint additions to the backlog. I'll use a Kanban Board for team tasks, but I won't generally place strict limitations on tasks per column.

I feel Scrumban works well for me for a few reasons. First, I can continue interacting with other teams using Scrum's artifacts and events, but I can relax the time-boxing requirements within the team. I find time-boxing to be one of the most challenging aspects of Scrum to make work with data science, as it's often the case that only a single team member knows how to solve a particular task. This renders it impossible to play the "planning poker" I mentioned briefly in chapter nine. (Here, the whole team uses cards with Fibonacci numbers to debate how long a task should take.) Even the one person who understands the task often has trouble estimating how long it will take.

Another challenge with Scrum is that, because it's so common with data science projects to hit roadblocks caused by missing data or untested technology, it's difficult not only to estimate required time, but also to schedule delivery to hit a specific Sprint end date. With Scrumban, you have the freedom to deliver results mid-Sprint (subject to project deadlines, of course).

Companies I've consulted for generally haven't minded when my teams don't adhere strictly to the Scrum framework. In fact, I find I tend to be the one promoting stricter adherence to project management rules than the companies themselves. In particular, I encourage team members to make our agreed project management methodology transparent by thoroughly documenting goals and progress on project tracking and documentation tools, which I'll introduce in the next section.

Tooling

We're very fortunate as data scientists to have at our disposal some great tools developed by software developers, for software developers. In this section, I'm going to use the Atlassian suite of tools to illustrate categories of project management tooling, not because Atlassian software is necessarily better, but because it's common enough to be familiar.

Project Tracking

Your new best friend is the software you'll use for tracking project tasks. This software will hold descriptions of the purpose, requirements, dependencies, progress and people involved with each of your tasks. Many teams use Trello or Atlassian's Jira for this.

> *Everyone asks how to pronounce "Jira," so I'm going to take a detour to explain. "Jira" is pronounced as the letter G ("jee"), plus "ra." This comes from "Gojira," which is Japanese for "Godzilla." You see, Jira was introduced to compete with Bugzilla, another piece of software—hence the play on words. Now you know, and you can go tell your colleagues.*

Whichever tool you use, your company will have an administrator who customizes it for your team. Hopefully your company also has an Agile coach who can guide you in using the software to facilitate your Agile methodology.

When you begin a new project, start by creating a corresponding epic in your tracking system. The epic will document key information about the project and will link to a number of smaller tasks in your product backlog. These smaller tasks should be sized so they'll take anywhere from several hours up to two or three weeks. I have templates I use for epics and tasks. (You can download them at dsianalytics.com/templates.)

Your project tracking tool is the place to assign tasks, record progress, upload supporting documentation, and tag people for tasks or comments. When you tag someone, your project tracking tool can notify that person by email, thus getting their attention.

The nice thing with tagging is that, by tagging someone in a comment, you've made a statement to that person and anyone viewing your task in the system. For example, if you need Jenny to create an account for you, you write a comment on the task that says something like "Requested @JennySmith to create account so I can continue." That comment has a date next to it. Two days later, you add a comment "Still waiting for @JennySmit …" Now you've got a paper trail of why your work isn't done yet.

As you continue to document progress for each task, you're also creating a public record of your work—along with reasons for any delays caused by dependencies. This record can be used in your ongoing stakeholder management, as I discussed in chapter nine.

Project Documentation

If project tracking is your best friend, the best friend of your business buddies will be the technology you use for project documentation. Typically, this will be something like a wiki. The Atlassian product with this functionality is called Confluence (this time not a Japanese word). Whereas the project tracking tool helps you plan and document your tasks, the project documentation system will be the shared material that remains after the tasks are done.

I generally copy many of my Sprint demo slides into the project documentation tool to make my presentations permanently available for stakeholders.

Code Repositories

You'll want to make disciplined use of a shared code repository, both for version control and for facilitating teamwork. Several commonly used code repositories exist, including Github, Gitlab and Atlassian's Bitbucket. I could say a lot about their functionality, but the subject quickly gets quite technical. Your company should already be using one or more of them.

How Data Science Project Management Differs from That of Software Developers

You'll benefit greatly from the tools and methods of software developers, but remember that the project management challenges you'll face as a data scientist will be different from theirs. Whereas Agile moved away from overly structured project management, data scientists often start with the opposite problem—a general lack of structure in their work.

Data science projects are generally open-ended, starting with only a vague goal. In fact, roughly one-third of all data science work can be classified as research and development.[26] If anything, data scientists need to **increase** the amounts of structure and documentation within their projects, so as to stay focused on delivering business results rather than getting bogged down in endless research or striving for overoptimized results.

Compared to IT projects, data science projects generally carry higher risks of failure, have vaguer KPIs and use nonstandard "Definitions of Done" (DoDs). In addition, data science end-to-end deliverables often require a broad range of skills: data discovery, ETL, feature generation, model fitting, production-quality coding, model deployment and continued monitoring—often employing streaming and/or cloud technologies.

Because of these differences—most notably the heavy emphasis on research, broad skill requirements and nonstandard deliverables—we data scientists need to adapt the methods used by software developers to serve our needs. The last three sections illustrate how we can accomplish that.

---

[26] Figure Eight. (2018). *Data scientist report 2018*. Figures are for the US market.

A Heavy Emphasis on Research

The following table lists project management challenges specifically related to the research aspect of data science, along with steps to help address them.

Challenge	Steps to Address
Research doesn't fit well with Scrum concepts of time-boxing or incremental delivery.	Adjust your methodology to fit the types of tasks, potentially using a Scrumban hybrid.
Data scientists may become absorbed in endless reading and research.	Set time limits on these tasks and require frequent reports on findings.
Stakeholders generally don't understand the risks and uncertainties of the research phase.	Increase the frequency of communication. Report intermediate, suboptimal and even failed efforts.

End-to-End Projects Require Broad Skill Sets

Similarly, we can modify how we construct and collaborate across teams.

Challenge	Steps to Address
Dependencies on different skills pull our projects toward a Waterfall approach.	Assemble team members with capabilities that span required skills.
Data scientists placed within technical teams often sit far from end users.	Include stakeholders in the RASCI, kickoff meeting and subsequent updates. Encourage frequent contact, as described earlier in this chapter.

Nonstandard Deliverables

Lastly, we can make accommodations for projects where our intermediate goal isn't to deliver functioning code.

Challenge	Steps to Address
Stakeholders expect linear progress toward a complete solution.	Clarify that deliverables may be data analysis or experimentation.
Our experiments frequently fail.	Clarify to stakeholders and to the team itself that "experiment failed" is a valid deliverable.
Traditional Definitions of Done (DoDs) aren't always relevant for data science projects.	Develop your own DoD. This could relate to breadth of research, testing or documentation of findings, rather than to coding elements such as unit test coverage.
Risks and delays inherent in data science projects can cause stakeholders to lose trust.	Educate stakeholders on project risks. Encourage the data scientists to deliver less-than-perfect iterations in a timely manner.

Ultimately, the process of tailoring existing methods and frameworks to best suit your situation is what modern project management is all about. So start with the foundation that's already been laid for you by software developers and other data scientists, but continue to experiment and refine ways of working so as to find what works best for you and your team. And always continue to develop your ways of working, because the system that works well for you today may need to be modified as your projects, and even team members, continue to change.

In Conclusion

Data scientists need to unlearn the perfectionism and thoroughness that served them so well earlier in life, embracing instead a drive to find shortcuts and partial solutions that will quickly deliver benefit in the areas most important to their organizations.

Even with this revised vision, the ambiguities of real-world data science make it very difficult to effectively scope and deliver larger projects over extended time periods. Your projects will have a much higher chance of success if you execute them in the right way: breaking them down into clearly defined tasks, delivering incremental value, and, above all, maintaining clear lines of communication with your end users.

Fortunately, the software development world has produced highly effective principles, frameworks and tooling to help in these areas. So choose a suitable project management framework; make it a point to develop PoCs, MVPs and pilots prior to full deployment; and learn how to better leverage existing project management and documentation software. But remember that data science differs significantly from software development, so you'll always need to find out which methods work best for your team.

Additional Reading

McGreal, D., & Jocham, R. (2018). *The professional product owner: Leveraging Scrum as a competitive advantage.* Addison-Wesley Professional.

The Agile Manifesto. https://agilemanifesto.org/. It's only 250 words, so why not read it?

Jurney, R. (2017). *Agile data science 2.0: Building full-stack data analytics applications with Spark.* O'Reilly Media. (Particularly the first chapter.)

For a comparison of Agile principles with principles followed by Lockheed Martin's Skunk Works Lab, which designed and built America's first jet fighter in only 143 days, see https://www.red-gate.com/blog/database-devops/real-origins-agile-manifesto, accessed Sept 4, 2000.

TOPIC SIX

• • • •

Careers

CHAPTER TWELVE

Planning a Career and Strengthening Your CV

I find myself often giving career advice to data scientists I meet in my role as a consultant and trainer, and I'd like to share some of that advice in this final chapter.

I won't give interviewing tips here or recommend specific specializations or companies, but I will give some principles for making yourself more marketable, and I'll help guide your thinking regarding career goals and which positions may suit you best. I'll also talk about how to go about pursuing those goals and positions.

What Is Your Goal?

The reason I can't offer you one-size-fits-all career advice is that there is no one-size-fits-all career; each of us has different values and ambitions. One person wants to develop cutting-edge ML technology, while another wants to eventually become a senior executive, perhaps managing a data science department within a large organization.

For example, ask yourself the following questions:

1. Would I prefer coding all day or meeting with others to solve business challenges—or perhaps a mixture of the two?

2. Would I rather be an individual contributor, a team leader or a senior executive who delegates as much as possible?

3. What's more important to me: salary, the type of work I do, or work-life balance?

4. Would I enjoy mastering a single technology or application, or would I rather build a broad, albeit more shallow, understanding of several topics?

Your answer to these questions will influence the roles you pursue and the skills you develop at the start of your career. But before going into detail about this, I want to mention some key principles that help almost all professionals advance toward the goals they choose.

Advancing Your Career

You've doubtless worked hard to earn a degree or acquire a certification. Although such in-class training provides a nice foundation for your CV, it's only the first step in making yourself marketable—and it may be less important than you'd expect in terms of landing jobs or getting promotions. Let's look at additional ways you can make yourself marketable and advance your career.

General Principles for Career Advancement

Regardless of whether you already have experience working as a data scientist or whether you've just finished a degree or training program, it's important that you develop the nontechnical dimensions that will influence your chances of getting a job offer. Here are five such dimensions that I've seen to be important.

1. **Networking**. Your professional network is one of your most important assets in building your career. Introductions from people in your network are the best way to get your foot in the door at companies or departments you're targeting. Your

network is also a great source of information for determining where you might or might not want to work.

How do you develop and maintain a strong professional network? Start by keeping in touch with former classmates and colleagues. Build new connections by attending conferences and meetups. Whenever you're at professional events, including internal company events, introduce yourself to new people, get their contact details, and send follow-up emails.

Use LinkedIn, but use it wisely. Don't simply spam random people with meaningless connection requests, and don't participate in online tirades. Instead, post and react to meaningful content. Follow people you respect and comment on their content as appropriate.

If you're just finishing school, contact older classmates who are already in the workforce. Ask your professors if they can refer you to former students who now work in areas or companies that interest you. Even without such an introduction, an alumni of your school is likely to be responsive if you reach out to them and mention that you're about to graduate from their alma mater and are looking for a first job. LinkedIn groups are a good way to find and contact such alumni.

One of the professionals who helped review the content of my first book was someone I'd met through a discussion on LinkedIn, although he lived halfway across the globe. Most of the projects I've done as a consultant have come to me because I maintained connections with people I'd initially had only casual contact with.

2. **Experience**. Make it a point to get experience in new areas whenever possible—new analytic methods, technologies, business applications or leadership roles. You'll find it very

difficult to get an interview for a role with responsibilities you have no experience carrying out, as hiring managers often place the highest value on past work experience. It's said that a company will prefer to hire the former CEO of a bankrupt company over a candidate with no CEO experience. Sometimes the business world values experience over success. As I mentioned in chapter four, you should push your manager to give you more responsibility rather than pushing for a higher salary. This will pay off in the long run.

3. **Recommendations**. Strong recommendations go a long way in helping you secure a position. A positive statement coming from someone else is much stronger than if it comes from you directly.

   You don't need to wait until you're asked to find references. You can actively solicit and publish references even when you're not interviewing. For example, ask a colleague or manager to post a recommendation on LinkedIn, or request permission to include their name as a reference on your CV or professional website.

   In choosing references, identify colleagues or managers who you sense have insight into and respect for your work. Ideally, they should have professional profiles that carry weight, such as managers or colleagues with extensive experience at well-known companies. Make sure your references can speak knowledgably about your work, or else they won't be credible when your potential employer contacts them. Also, try to find people who understand how to give good references. If your reference is a poor communicator, very junior or generally critical of everyone, they may not leave a good impression of you.

One other point regarding LinkedIn. Avoid connecting with people who are likely to speak negatively of you. If you and the hiring manager share a connection, the hiring manager is likely to approach that connection in private to ask their opinion of you.

4. **Pedigree**. Find ways to associate yourself with something reputable. The reputation of your school will help in landing your first job. The reputation of your past employers will help in landing future jobs (so try to land your first job with a reputable company, regardless of salary). If you've worked on a high-profile project, whether at work or as a contributor to open source, this will also enhance your pedigree. You may even choose to mention nontechnical achievements. If you were an Olympic athlete (I wasn't, but a former colleague at eBay was), mention this on your CV. Whatever helps the hiring manager make a positive association with you will make you more attractive as a candidate.

5. **Mobility**. If you want to progress quickly in your career, be prepared to move as opportunities arise in other departments, companies or geographies. Although moving where you live may be challenging at certain stages of life (such as when you have a child or partner in school), it can also be a fantastic opportunity to broaden your horizons. A word of warning— some people are attracted to the idea of moving to a new city or country, only to get cold feet and back out after the job offer arrives. Hiring managers know this, and it's a tremendous waste of their time. As with any application process, you should prepare a convincing explanation as to why you want the position. In the case of mobility, research the new location and be prepared to explain during the interview why you're excited about relocating.

Some of these five may be challenging to develop at the start of your career, but you'll have opportunities to develop experience and pedigree in particular as you accumulate work experience.

Enhancing Your CV While Working

Once you've started your first job, work to demonstrate that you're a good communicator (chapters six and seven) and that you can handle responsibility (chapters eight and nine). Remember that the person you most need to impress is your direct manager, so concentrate at first on understanding what they expect and then meeting those expectations. Remember, your success depends on doing not what you think is a good job but what your manager thinks is a good job. Also, consider that it may take a year or more before you've earned the trust of your new manager, so don't take that trust for granted, and don't assume your manager should give you the benefit of the doubt before you've proven yourself. Use the stakeholder management principles I wrote about in chapter nine to help you earn and keep their trust, especially during the first critical months of your job.

As you progress in your work experience, continue to strengthen your CV in the following two ways:

1. **Build more experience**. I mentioned how companies look for past experience when they fill positions. Sometimes a little experience on your CV will be enough to get your foot in the door for that position.

   While you're in a job, get experience in as many areas as possible. For example, if you work primarily in digital marketing, try to get involved with a financial forecasting or fraud detection project. Do a PoC in natural language processing, image recognition or time series analysis.

If you're interested in applying for more senior positions in the future, try to get experience now as a people manager, a team leader or, at the very least, as a project leader.

Recruiting is not an exact science. You may be extremely talented, hard-working and responsible, but such traits are difficult to measure. Because so many interviewers are unable to accurately assess skill levels and unwilling to contact references, it's possible that an "experienced" candidate who has done a terrible job in the past is given preference over a more competent candidate with no experience.

Realizing the dependence some recruiters have on keywords, you've probably considered packing your CV with technical terms so your profile will show up more often in recruiters' searches. But keyword stuffing is a two-edged sword. My advice is never to fake expertise. You can choose to mention a technology even when you have very limited experience with it, but be candid when asked about the depth of your experience.

I've interviewed hundreds of data science applicants over the years. To vet them, I typically pick a topic listed on their resume, ask for a self-assessment of how well they know it, and then follow up with pointed technical questions. Often, the candidate claims expert knowledge but fails to demonstrate even basic understanding. This is an automatic fail. If, however, the applicant admits to only a basic skill level in that area, I feel more confident of their integrity and self-awareness. These are the candidates I'm willing to hire.

2. **Start keeping score**. Find ways to positively quantify your achievements. Here's a piece of invaluable advice I received

a few years back: don't load your resume with generic phrases that could apply to anyone—phrases like "team player who always gives 100% and thinks outside the box." State the specifics of what you've achieved and do that in measurable ways. For example: "I led a team of six data scientists to design and deploy to production a churn reduction model that increased customer retention by 18% year over year, saving the company an estimated $1.4 million over the first two years."

Continue to add additional experiences and achievement metrics to your CV and especially to your LinkedIn profile, even when you aren't actively looking for a new role. This habit will remind you to keep seeking new types of experience and to measure the quantifiable impact of each new project (as I discussed in chapter eight).

Making Decisions

Now that I've talked about some ways to advance your career, let's focus on a few career decisions you'll need to make.

First and foremost, you need to be honest with yourself about what's really important to you. Reflect on the four goal questions listed earlier in this chapter. Be willing to sacrifice in the areas you've decided aren't as important. For example, don't take a high-stress position on Wall Street if you aren't prepared to work evenings and weekends, or if you really want to develop healthcare applications. Don't take a position at certain prestigious but generally secretive companies if you want to continue publishing research in your field.

Once you've clarified your priorities, you can begin taking deliberate steps in your career, starting with targeting your first job.

Deciding on a First Job

If your goal is to **rise in seniority**, eventually becoming a senior data science manager at a prestigious company, you'll want your first job to be at a prestigious company. For technical work, this could mean one of the FAANG companies (Facebook, Apple, etc.). Experience at such companies will generally look good on your CV, although there may be drawbacks in terms of your professional development. In such a large organization, you'll likely find yourself in a specialized role with limited overview of the larger organization. A role at a smaller company, on the other hand, would more likely provide you with broader experience across multiple business units.

Also, while it's true that working at a well-known tech company provides the opportunity to work closely with especially capable colleagues, many equally talented data scientists have chosen to work at smaller companies. So don't assume that the best work or the best people are always found at the best-known companies.

Be honest with yourself if your real ambition is to be an executive rather than a data scientist. In this case, you'll do better applying to a management consulting firm, such as McKinsey or BCG. It's a very different career path, especially at the start.

If your goal is **work-life balance and stability**, you'll want to find out how the company scores in this area before accepting a job offer. Try to get an idea as to how long typical workdays are, how frequently people work evenings or weekend, and what employee turnover rates are. And if you want geographic stability, choose a job in an area with multiple employers close by. Such locations give you the option to change jobs without relocating.

If your goal is to **specialize in a subfield of ML**, find a company with an established department doing what you want to do, preferably one with ties to a strong university, where professors and graduate students can support your work. In particular, don't take a first job as the founding member of a new innovation team, as you'll have neither the support nor the mandate to do advanced research in such a role.

If you'd prefer to get **exposure to a broad range of industries**, consider starting in a technical consulting company. Not only will you have the chance to change projects without changing companies, you'll also rub shoulders with colleagues working across a broad spectrum of projects and sectors. Such companies may also offer more training opportunities (but ask specifically about this when you interview).

Another alternative is to **join a startup**. This will generally put you in a high-energy environment and provide the broadest opportunity to stretch yourself in all sorts of directions. But realize that the payoff in a startup is uncertain, and you may not get the chance to use or develop specialized skills. Working in a startup may also require extensive overtime.

Disillusionment

Once you start your first job as a data scientist, you'll experience what it's like to work in what has been termed "the sexiest job of the 21st century." The hype is one thing, the reality something else. It's possible that you'll become disillusioned.

There are several reasons why data scientists grow discontented in their roles. As I wrote in chapter one, many companies simply don't know how to put the skills of data scientists to good use. In that chapter, I described companies rushing to get on the bandwagon, purchasing technologies and hiring data scientists, yet with no clear applications in mind. These data scientists invariably become frustrated when they aren't given clear direction and don't have a chance to apply the skills they've worked so hard to develop.

Even when goals are clear, data scientists may be assigned tasks that don't fit their training. The following graph illustrates this point. It shows the results of a recent survey in which data scientists indicated how they view the activities they're typically assigned.[27]

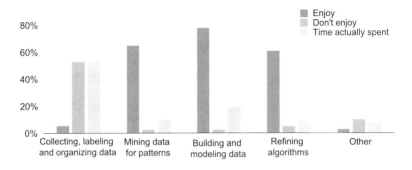

Figure 64. Data scientists' enjoyment of their most common tasks

As you can see in this graph, the data wrangling tasks—although least enjoyed—took the most time. Respondents spent relatively little time on the actual data mining and model building—the tasks they were trained to do. This disconnect between expected and realized tasks may explain why so many data scientists decide to change jobs.

On the topic, I'd like to point out that it's not necessary to assign so much data wrangling work to data scientists. Think back to chapter eight, where I described the process for scoping out necessary resources at the very start of a project. As a project leader specifies the project RASCI, they should estimate the amount of data wrangling required and secure the support of dedicated data engineers. This will free the data scientists to focus on tasks for which they're best suited and most enjoy—mining for insights, building models and refining algorithms.

Deciding to Change Jobs

As a data scientist, it's likely you'll change jobs often. In the survey referenced above, thirty-five percent of data scientists responded that they'd been in their roles for less than two years. Although a job in a traditional industry—such as a retail bank, insurance company or large manufacturer—may allow you to remain comfortably in one team for years or even decades, many companies—particularly tech companies—evolve very rapidly, leading to high employee churn. In such companies, you may witness near-continuous reorganizations and a high rate of staff turnover. Even in more traditional companies, the newer data science roles may appear and disappear rapidly. So don't be surprised if you find that your position has changed drastically from what it was when you were hired a few years or even months previously.

> *I myself witnessed multiple reorganizations during the four years I worked at eBay. My reporting line changed, on average, once every six months. After only two years, I had already been in that office longer than probably half of my colleagues. And I wouldn't say that eBay was unusual in that respect. I've known data scientists who have changed jobs annually over the past four to five years.*

The advantage of such a high churn rate for you as a data scientist is that you can quickly build a very wide network of former colleagues. Remember that your network is one of your most important assets, both in getting your foot in the door for new positions and for hearing firsthand what it's like to work at other companies. Your network may also alert you to new job openings even before they're published.

If you reach the point where you decide to look around for a new job, your network is the best place to start. Reach out to your contacts, and not just the ones in data science. You can tell them directly that you're looking around, or you can choose to be more discreet, asking about how their work is, what type of work they're doing and if their data science team is growing. You might also ask them if they can introduce you to others they know who might be hiring.

Your second-best option for finding a new position is to work with an independent recruiter (a "headhunter"). The advantage of working with a headhunter is that they can give you additional insights into the companies and positions they work with, which will in turn help you refine your applications for those positions. Headhunters can also help promote your application to the hiring manager or internal recruiter. In addition, some positions will only be accessible via designated headhunters, although this tends to be true only of the more senior positions.

But be careful when working with headhunters. Although some are experienced professionals with high levels of integrity, others are dubious at best. The worst headhunters won't understand anything about your field. They'll spam companies with your CV without your consent and waste your time trying to match you to positions that are completely not what you're looking for. Those headhunters may also not respect your confidentiality, disclosing details of your job search to others without your consent.

If you're considering working with a headhunter you don't know personally, check their work experience (on LinkedIn) and ask within your network to learn about the reputation of their company. Remember that most positions will be available through several headhunters simultaneously, so don't be afraid that you might lose an opportunity by not working with a headhunter you don't trust.

If you apply directly on a company website, add a well-thought-out cover letter. Explain why the position interests you and why you think you'll be a good fit.

Internal recruiters will often reach out to candidates based on their LinkedIn profiles, so make sure your profile is up to date and gives a strong impression of your skills, experience and professionalism (including headshot, grammar and spelling).

Obviously, there are many additional challenges to the process of changing jobs: asking current colleagues for references, asking for time off for interviews, negotiating counteroffers and navigating noncompete clauses. It's difficult to give general advice for these challenges, as they depend on your current situation and on your preference in navigating such gray areas.

Deciding to Change Roles

At some point, you'll probably be ready for more responsibility and a higher pay grade. People generally want to get promoted, although this isn't always the case. Your first promotions probably won't change your responsibilities much—you'll simply be progressing from junior to senior data scientist. But you'll need to consider if you really want to move further into a management position.

A promotion to a management role is more significant, bringing more responsibility and often a complete change in daily tasks. Becoming a manager isn't without its drawbacks; technical people often find themselves frustrated by the exchange of hands-on work for back-to-back meetings, budgeting responsibilities and increased office politics. And once you've stopped doing hands-on work, you can easily get left behind by the rapid advancements in technology and data science algorithms. On the flip side, a management position generally offers insight into and influence over a broader range of technical projects, as well as deeper insight into the business drivers of data science projects. As a manager, you also have the opportunity to choose and mentor a new cohort of data scientists within your organization.

Some data science managers do keep themselves involved in the technical work, splitting their time between leadership responsibilities and hands-on tasks. This may continue until you're promoted to senior management, at which point you'll probably find it impossible to take time away from your extended management responsibilities to do hands-on work.

If you're given the chance to take a more senior role involving no hands-on work, consider carefully whether or not that's what you really want.

Deciding to Go Freelance

At a certain point in your career—although probably not at the beginning—you may consider venturing out on your own as an independent contractor (a freelancer) rather than continuing to work as a company employee.

Quite a number of data scientists I've spoken with would prefer to work freelance rather than as permanent employees. These people cite the potential for higher income and more flexibility, or they're tired of working under a manager or dealing with office politics. Some people I know have taken the leap, only to return to the corporate workforce a few months or years later. Some return to permanent positions because they miss the sense of ownership and comradery that comes with being an internal employee and working on your own company's projects. Many don't enjoy the task of "selling" themselves to new clients every time a freelance project ends. But many others thrive as freelancers, and they continue at it for years.

Which choice is right for you? I generally give the following advice when people tell me they're considering switching to freelance:

1. **Make sure you have a good financial buffer** before you leave your current job, as it's not unusual for freelancers to spend

several months between assignments. A higher daily wage when you do have an assignment compensates for periods without work. Although you can conceivably invoice in six months what you would earn as an internal employee in one year, remember that a freelancer also needs to pay health insurance, disability insurance, office costs and administrative costs. In addition, a freelancer needs to build up their own pension (plus social security in the US), and all sick days and holidays remain unpaid.

2. **Make yourself very visible**. Be more active on LinkedIn, attend and speak at conferences, tell all your past colleagues that you've gone freelance, and update your LinkedIn headline to reflect your new status. While you're between projects, update your LinkedIn profile to indicate "open for new projects."

3. **Network with other freelancers**. When I first transitioned to freelance, I was surprised at how open the freelance community is. Many freelancers will share leads if they're fully booked themselves. And they'll often tell each other what rates they're currently charging clients, providing valuable benchmarks.

4. **Contact headhunters specializing in freelancers** (taking into account my previous words of caution regarding them). Most freelancers I know are placed through such specialized headhunters. They'll generally charge the freelancer a fee somewhere between ten and thirty percent of the rate billed to the client. But watch out; most won't tell you the rate the client is actually paying them, and they may be skimming off fifty percent of the rate charged to the client.

Again, network with other freelancers to find out who to work with and what rates are reasonable in your market.

Typically, you would wait to make this career move until after you've accumulated enough experience to be able to market yourself as a competent freelancer with a strong track record and a reasonable set of recommendations. Once you're ready, here are three ways you can sell your services:

1. **Consulting**. As a consultant, you can work on projects where you're paid to give advice—typically part-time or over a short period. You can generally charge the highest rates for this type of work.

2. **Project delivery**. In this capacity, you're paid to work independently to deliver results. Quite often, you'll do the project with a team of consultants. This is typical work for a company like Deloitte or Accenture.

3. **Staff augmentation**. Here you function almost as an internal employee. The company assigns you tasks within a larger project that the company itself is managing. Staff augmentation is typically the lowest paid freelance work, but it's also the easiest to land. From what I've seen, staff augmentation projects can last for several years.

Most freelancers I know here in The Netherlands work in staff augmentation. Consulting projects are more difficult to find and require more seniority. There are fewer staff augmentation opportunities in countries such as the US, where labor laws allow companies to let employees go much more easily. With these looser labor laws, companies are free to rapidly scale their internal workforce up or down and have less need for freelancers to supplement their internal staff. In such environments, freelancers are under more pressure to deliver incremental value.

Whichever path you choose, going freelance doesn't need to be a one-time decision. Many data scientists work freelance for a few years and then take another internal role.

In Conclusion

It's an exciting time to work in data science. You have a world of opportunities to choose from, whether it be in traditional firms, newer tech companies or fresh startups. But you'll need to stretch beyond your technical training to enable each next step in your career. You'll need to develop and leverage a range of business skills—to gain the trust and support of people around you, to communicate clearly and convincingly and to identify and deliver results with clear business value.

There are many career paths to take as a data scientist, so consider what's important for you in your next position or company and, ultimately, in your career. As you continue to develop your business skills, they'll open up more professional opportunities for you, helping you to succeed in whichever path you do choose. Hopefully, these skills will also make your work as a data scientist that much more enjoyable.

Glossary

AutoML: A tool that automates model building, typically iterating through many simple models to arrive at one with the best fit.

Accuracy: A measure of model effectiveness computed as the fraction of instances correctly classified.

Business Intelligence (BI): The business area that specializes in technologies and processes for collecting data and making it available for reporting and analysis.

Capital Expense: An accounting term encompassing expenses for long-term benefit, such as hardware purchases.

Cognitive Load: A term in psychology referring to the amount of mental resources used.

Cost per Click (CPC): A costing method in digital marketing where advertisers are charged based on the number of clicks on their advertisements.

Cost per Mil (CPM): A costing method in digital marketing where advertisers are charged based on the number of times their advertisements are displayed on web pages.

F1 Score: A measure of model effectiveness that combines both precision and recall according to a specific formula.

Gatekeeper: A person who's able to restrict or grant access to a leader or decision maker in an organization.

GDPR (General Data Protection Regulation): A regulation placing strict requirements on how organizations use and protect the personal data of members of the European Union.

Inter-Quartile Range (IQR): The width between the first and third quartiles of a data set.

Key Performance Indicator (KPI): A metric used to track an important aspect of performance; e.g., net revenue, number of customers, customer churn rate, etc.

Mean Absolute Percentage Error (MAPE): A measure of model effectiveness. It's the average of the absolute values of the error terms divided by the corresponding data values.

Mean Squared Error (MSE): A measure of model effectiveness. It's the average of the squares of the model error terms.

Mergers and Acquisitions (M&A): A general term used to describe various transactions where assets or whole companies are acquired or merged.

Minimum Viable Product (MVP): A usable product providing no more than the minimum required functionality. The classic example is that a skateboard could be an MVP, but one wheel of a car could not.

OKR (Objectives and Key Results): A goal-setting framework emphasizing collaboration and the achievement of high-level objectives through the targeting of certain key results.

Operational Expenses: An accounting term encompassing expenses that represent the continuing costs of doing business.

Outlier: In statistics, a data point that is (perhaps subjectively) deemed to be outside of the normal range of values.

Pilot: A limited-scope deployment in production. For example, a pilot might be deployed in only one geography or for a limited number of customers.

Precision: A measure of model effectiveness computed as the fraction of retrieved instances that are actual instances.

Private Equity (PE) Firms: Investment management companies that invest in companies and financial assets that aren't publicly traded.

Proof of Concept (PoC): A work done to demonstrate feasibility. For example, the PoC may train a simplified model on a manually selected subset of data, or it may set up a simplified pipeline to demonstrate connectivity between systems. The PoC doesn't need to produce something of actual use.

Recall: A measure of model effectiveness computed as the fraction of instances that are retrieved.

REST API: An architectural style often used by computers communicating across a network. REST is an acronym for REpresentational State Transfer.

Stakeholder: A person with an interest in or dependency on the project.

Type 1 Error: False positives.

Type 2 Error: False negatives.

Use Case: A complete specification for a solution—what you should build and exactly how it should behave in all situations.

User Story: A brief description of the business challenge and goal. The user story focuses on what may be called "the happy path" or the typical user flow. It doesn't (yet) specify what happens in unusual situations.

Venture Capital (VC) Firms: Private equity firms that generally focus on high-growth (and often higher risk) investments.

Web Service: An application or data source that's accessible over the Internet using a standard protocol.

Acknowledgments

Quite a number of professionals around the globe have provided some form of specific input for this book over the past months, and I'm very grateful for their input. I'd like to particularly thank my four beta readers: Timo Bohm, Warner de Jong, Alireza Kashani, and Andre Sharapov, who each read through the entire first draft of this book in a short period of time and provided extremely valuable feedback, sometimes prompting me to rewrite entire chapters.

I'd like to thank my developmental editor, Kristen Havens, for many valuable contributions as she helped develop the larger narrative while maintaining a focus on the readers' perspective. It's been a pleasure to work through this project together, despite the nine-hour time difference. Thanks also to my copy editor, Carl Quesnel, who amazed me with how quickly he was able to significantly improve the manuscript; to Heather Pendley, for her rapid proofreading; and to Michelle Guiliano, for constructing the index. Thanks to Nick Zelinger and Rebecca Finkel, the Coloradans who helped design the cover and interior layouts, and a big thanks to Justin Mincks, who performed some amazing graphic design magic to convert my Microsoft files into vector files.

Lastly, I'd like to thank the many data scientists who have participated in training sessions I've given over the years and who have shared with me their own experiences as data scientists. Your questions, comments and feedback have helped to shape the content of this book.

About the Author

David Stephenson is a consulting data scientist, trainer, and occasional chair of the PAW ML conference series. Since receiving his PhD from Cornell University, he has worked in a variety of industries, including several years as Head of Global Business Analytics for eBay Classifieds Group, where he worked with teams of data scientists and engineers spread across six continents. He has held part-time faculty positions at the University of Pennsylvania and the University of Amsterdam.

David is also the author of *Big Data Demystified: How to Use Big Data, Data Science and AI to Make Better Business Decisions and Gain Competitive Advantage,* published in 2018 by Financial Times Press. That book, written for nontechnical executives, provides a high-level overview of key terms and concepts, followed by several chapters describing how to create and develop a data science program.

Although he currently lives in The Netherlands, David still tells everyone he meets that he's from Pennsylvania.

You can contact him at dstephenson@dsianalytics.com.

Index

Page numbers in **bold** reference figures and their captions.